Fight to Clear
Barry George
of the Jill Dando Murder

MIKE BURKE

authorHOUSE®

AuthorHouse™
1663 Liberty Drive
Bloomington, IN 47403
www.authorhouse.com
Phone: 1-800-839-8640

Published by AuthorHouse   06/08/2012

ISBN: 978-1-4685-8586-5 (sc)
ISBN: 978-1-4685-8587-2 (hc)
ISBN: 978-1-4685-8588-9 (e)

Contents

Acknowledgements

I would like to express my thanks to the following for their help and advice.

Margaret Renn, Michael Mansfield QC. Dr Susan Young. Jeremy Moore.

Willie O Dea TD for his help and support. MP's John McDonnell and Jeremy Corbyn for their help and support.

Mick and Joy Lynch for kick-starting the JfB campaign, and Victoria for all the tea.

Pat Reynolds, Andy Parr, Mick Gilgunn, Scott Lomax, Martin and Vicky Jeremiah.

Tanya and Louise from Rough Justice.

Raphael Rowe, Kristen and the Panorama team.

David Perrin, James Cohen and the Cutting Edge team.

Ann Moneypenny. Hazel Keirle. Paddy Hill.

Don Hale. Don Shaw. Christopher Parr.

David James Smith for his insight, advice and patience.

All those who gave their names for the 'Concerned' list and those who for professional reasons could not.

Colin Horrabin and all the Guest Book contributors including the negative ones. Criticism can be helpful.

And for all those who helped Barry George and our families with advice, encouragement or support over the eight years of the struggle.

Prologue

'All parties in George to court number one' came the call over the tannoy. That's odd I thought as we jumped up slightly startled. It was Friday August 1-2008, lunchtime had just ended and I was surprised at the early call. The jury was not supposed to have deliberated during lunch but perhaps they simply wanted to ask a question before going home for the weekend. As we made our way from the Old Baileys cafeteria down the stairs to the famous courtroom we heard that the jury were coming in, there was a verdict. This was shocking, very like the awful day in 2001 when we were again unexpectedly called from the cafeteria. I hurriedly sent Scott Lomax a text which I had prepared earlier, saying 'verdict come in quick'. I sat between MOJO's Serj Sinclair and Tanya while Michelle sat on the far side of Tanya. The courtroom was packed but the public gallery was almost empty apart from Scott and a court official. 'Be upstanding' the court clerk ordered and the Hon Justice Griffith Williams came in, bowed and sat. He then asked the press to go easy on the jury who had just made a very tough decision. He ordered that nobody was to leave the courtroom until he said so.

The tension was just awful as the jury filed in. I looked at their faces as I had done in 2001 hoping to see a smile but again there was nothing. They all seemed to be looking down at their feet. It did not look at all good and Serj and I exchanged worried glances. Tanya grabbed Michelle and my hands and we braced ourselves for the worst.

'Have you reached a verdict' asked the judge?

'Yes' said the grim looking foreman.

Do you find the defendant guilty or not guilty of the murder of Jill Dando?'

'Not guilty' said the foreman loudly.

I slumped in disbelief as Michelle and Tanya jumped up punching the air yelling *YES* and a court official yelled 'sit down'. Up above us Scott applauded in the public gallery. It was unbelievable, more shocking than the guilty verdict seven years earlier and I don't think we quite took it in. Barry just stood silently in the dock until the judge told him he was free to go. His solicitor Jeremy Moore couldn't stop smiling as he told me that I should have had more faith in the defence. It was the best moment in many years and the end of an eight year battle by Michelle, I and our fellow supporters to get justice for Barry.

On April 26 1999 I was surprised to hear the news on my car radio that the BBC TV presenter Jill Dando had been mugged, possibly stabbed and was believed to have died. 'O God, another one?' I thought. I was comparing her death to that three years earlier of Veronica Guerin who was shot a number of times as she drove into Dublin following a court appearance in Naas. I later saw that Jill had been shot, not stabbed.

Up to that the big news that spring was the NATO intervention in the then Serbian province of Kosovo. I would listen to the accounts of the bombers leaving RAF airfields on my radio while walking with my dog Shannon, and of the so called warlord Arkan who took his private army the 'Tiger's' down to Kosovo. I never dreamed that those news stories would assume any significance for me and my family in the years ahead.

I did not take any particular interest in the Dando murder then, I was more concerned with the declining health of my mother who was ill. She died in September of that year.

In early May 2000 I visited my sister Margaret in London as part of my summer holidays. Her son Barry had called to see me on the day I arrived, but had left before I got there. Later I mentioned that to one of my brothers who explained that Barry was a little uptight as he was getting a bit of hassle from the police over the Jill Dando murder. I was puzzled, why would the police be interested in him, surely he wasn't involved? Could he have done it? 'No no of course not, but the silly prat has been going around talking about the murder and has got the attention of the police'.

A couple of days later Margaret told me that the police had recently questioned Barry in her presence and had also searched her house. I felt glad that I hadn't been there. Barry called around in the evening before Coronation Street ended. Margaret's lifelong friend Annie was chatting away as she does while I was engrossed in Corrie. After a time I realised that something had changed and then I realised that Annie had stopped talking. I looked over to her and was a little surprised to see her sitting in silence, which is unusual. Barry had a meal and watched a film on Channel 5, a rather nasty film about a woman who was trapped with a murderous psychotic gunman in a camper van. At one stage she managed to get hold of a gun but could not bring herself to shoot the man in the back. 'She knows what to do but she can't do it' said Barry. That sent a shiver down my spine and I stole a sideways glance at him wondering for a moment would he be able to do it, was I sitting next to a murderer? But though I thought he looked a little tense he otherwise seemed much the same as ever and I dismissed the possibility. I didn't mention the police and neither did he. I wasn't aware then that he was being followed around by a team of police. I did fear that he might ask me for a drive to Ireland when I was going home the next morning but to my relief he didn't.

I had last met him in November 1998 when we had discussed his interest in computers. He spoke then of his hopes of doing a university course boasting that he would be the only one in the family to have a degree. I got the impression that he hoped the course might have the end result of him becoming a pop star or performing on TV. As I said goodbye to him that night I joked 'the next time I see you, you will probably be on the box'. He looked puzzled and I repeated myself. He still looked puzzled and then Margaret said 'on the box, the telly'. Barry laughed in relief explaining that he thought I had said 'in the box', meaning in a coffin. Now it was my turn to be puzzled.

In the early summer of 1999 I spoke to him briefly on the phone. He told me that the university course was on hold and that he had curvature of the spine.

May 2000

It is dusk as I approach my front gate. Shannon, my Red Setter comes out on to the road to welcome me. Damn, Tom must have left the gate open. The house is in darkness but as I walk towards the door I become aware that there is somebody inside with Tom, something's not quite right. Looking behind me I see that there is a man at the gate but he shouldn't be there. He seems to be doing something to the gate, maybe trying to steal it.

I awoke with a start, it was just a silly dream but I felt disturbed and couldn't settle again, so I had a cup of tea. The dream was over, the nightmare lay ahead.

A couple of weeks after I had returned from my London holiday SKY News reported that police were confident of making a breakthrough in the Jill Dando murder investigation. I told my brother Tom that Barry had been questioned, and he laughed loudly at the idea. It just seemed too ridicules to him. But the speculation on Sky was gaining momentum and news of an arrest came on Thursday May 25. Again I tried to warn Tom, saying I hoped it wasn't Barry. Again he laughed, but I was uneasy, though not seriously worried. The next morning I started work at 11.05. I listened to the news on RTE Radio 1 at 11.00. They announced that an unemployed musician from Fulham was the man who was arrested, and they gave his name as Barry Bulsara, aged 40. I had never heard the name Bulsara but I realised that it just had to be our Barry. I tried to concentrate on my job for the rest of the day but my head was in turmoil. Even though I had partly expected it, the news hit me like a bombshell. On my break I tuned in as usual to the Joe Duffy radio phone-in on RTE 1. 'You met Bulsara', he began. It being a Friday Joe was having a bit of a laugh, and I thought he seemed to think it funny to hear a couple of people speak of having 'met Bulsara'. I really felt like grabbing a phone and letting rip but fortunately I managed to remain calm, at least on the outside. Of course Joe wasn't to know that Barry had family in Ireland, and emotion may have clouded my judgement but I was absolutely furious feeling that a laugh was being had at our expense.

I got home from work at 19.30. My ex directory phone rang, and a man with a coarse English accent claiming to be from the Daily Express asked if I was Bulsara's uncle. 'Who is Bulsara' I asked innocently? 'The geezer who was arrested for the Dando murder' he explained. I feigned ignorance and told him he had the wrong Burke, and he rang off. I then phoned Barry's Sister Michelle and she told me that she had already spoken to her mother about it. Tom then came in and I warned him not to answer the phone, explaining that Barry was under arrest for the murder. He swore as the realisation that I was not joking finally hit him. Just then the man from the Express phoned back and Tom answered. He began to talk, saying 'we don't want to know anything . . .' at which point I dived to the floor and pulled the plug from the wall socket.

Later on I phoned Barry's mother, who was by now under siege by the media at her house in East Acton. We discussed what might happen if Barry was charged. When we had finished our conversation I had to disconnect the phone again to stop it ringing. Margaret was like a prisoner in her house for a week and neighbours would hand her shopping to her over the garden fence.

The reporters arrived on Saturday morning before I left for work. I could not hide from them and decided it was probably best to appear polite. Richard Allewyn from the Daily Mail called along with a photographer. They wanted photographs of Barry. Richard asked me about Barry and I answered as honestly as I could. I said that I feared that the police might *conveniently* find some forensic evidence. He asked what I meant and I replied 'we all know our history, don't we?' I had seen or read that the police were digging in Barry's garden and were probing the cavities of his walls in a search for forensic evidence. I was thinking of what happened to the Birmingham Six, Guildford Four and McGuire Seven and wondered if something similar would happen to Barry. Shannon then walked up showing off a big bone she was gnawing and planted a friendly muddy paw on the knee of Richard's neatly pressed trousers. As they left I noticed Richard looking curiously at the latch of the front gate which I had painted in the colours of the Irish Tricolour.

Later, on my way home on a meal break I saw the Irish Mirror. 'HE's IRISH' the front page screamed. It named Barry's mother and where she came from. It mentioned my long dead father and where he worked. The detail was amazing. It was a wet stormy day. As I prepared to return to work the phone rang just as a huge flash of lightening struck the ground near my house followed by an enormous clap of thunder causing me to jump in fright. A relative was phoning, innocently asking me if I had any news, pretending she didn't know. I stalled her for the moment swearing as I saw a large umbrella passing my window and under it an Irish Mirror reporter. I spoke to him briefly, and unfortunately he noticed my work logo on my shirt. Shannon was traumatised by all the strange events and it took her a few weeks to settle again while life for the rest of us was changed forever.

[In an article in the Telegraph by Sally Pook and John Steel (which I read many years later) Barry's Fulham neighbours expressed shock and disbelief that he should have been arrested. He was described as a familiar face in the local pubs and shops sometimes dressed in a vest in the style of Queen's Freddie Mercury. One man described him as harmless saying, 'everyone in Fulham knows him as Thomas. He's known to all the shopkeepers as a bit of an oddball but he's harmless. You could even say he's loveable. Thomas is just Thomas. To convince me he killed Jill Dando the police would have to show me the gun and the blood. He had a fixation for Freddie Mercury but I never heard him mention Jill Dando.']

On Sunday 28 the men from the mail called again. Richard Allewyn said that his editor had authorised him to offer 'substantial' money for my photos of Barry. I refused to deal, saying that it would be like taking blood money. They then went to my elderly relatives a few miles away and had tea and apple pie.

Tom later told me that they called back some time later again trying to get some photos. Their meeting with my elderly relatives was later published but my comments were not.

I drove to Dublin on that Sunday. At Hammersmith police station the clock was ticking for the police who were questioning Barry, and the news reports kept saying that time was running out. I thought that if he was guilty he would surely have cracked by now. My hopes were rising but as I drove into Borris in Ossery at 20.00 they were dashed by the breaking news, he had been charged with the murder of Jill Dando.

On Monday the Irish Mirror reported where I worked and so I had to tell my bosses about the situation. They advised staff not to discuss the matter with the press.

That evening four reporters approached me as I was parking in the compound. One asked me if Michael Burke was back yet. By coincidence another Michael Burke was standing nearby and I was tempted to point to him, but realised that he would probably then point back to me. So I just said I didn't know and advised the reporter to go ask George the security man, who promptly ordered them off site. Will the real Michael Burke please stand up?

As I left the compound I donned glasses and my raincoat as a photographer was standing outside. Another driver was approaching and shouted 'hi Mike, I didn't know you wore glasses.' The photographer turned to look as I jumped into my car and sped away.

I drove home quickly, parked my car behind my house and padlocked the gate. The reporters were close behind and they waited around for a few hours, but though they spoke with neighbours they did not call to my gate or door. One neighbour told them to go eff off, and he called the Guards who asked them to leave. I was about to walk over the hills to go for a pint when the neighbour called to tell me that the coast was clear and so I was able to walk the road unhindered.

On Tuesday in the works canteen a few drivers were chatting. 'I see they got some local nutter for Jill Dando's murder,' Rob said. I froze and there was a deathly silence leaving poor Rob puzzled at the unusual lack of a reply or wisecrack from anybody.

When I got home I put a notice on the porch door saying **No Photos No Story So Don't Offer.** I then took Shannon for her walk. A helicopter flew low over the house causing me to duck back in to get my hat and glasses. I was getting paranoid. As we walked through the fields I wondered what I should do, it was fight or flight time. I chose fight, deciding that I would not bury my head in the sand. I would try to support Barry in the assumption that he was innocent. It was to be an unpopular decision but Barry is a relative and as deserving of my support as any other. I also knew that he would not have any great family support beyond sympathy and he would need help. I can't say that I felt greatly sympathetic towards him in an emotional way though for a time I would wake up early in the morning trying to make sense of it all.

One day Tom told me that a reporter from the Limerick Post called. She sat on her car bonnet, notebook in hand and made a note of the notice in the porch. Tom did not oblige by going out but Shannon did. Suddenly she gave a loud deep bark from inside the gate, the reporter leapt from the bonnet, jumped into her car and fled. But she managed to speak to some neighbours and wrote a half page report for her paper based on the note I had displayed in the porch.

One day a couple of weeks after Barry's arrest I arrived home in the middle of the day and Shannon really did come out on to the road to welcome me. My gate had been left partly open by a reporter who Tom thought was from the Daily Express. Do dreams come true?

Some relatives would wonder why I had not mentioned anything to them upon my return from London. But the reality is that I thought that there was nothing of importance to mention, as I had dismissed any thought that Barry might have had anything to do with the murder.

I am as mercenary as most people and at one stage I was tempted to cash in using my photos of Barry. One summers evening I arrived home from work and thought I detected my mother's presence in the house. I was puzzled and a little disturbed and actually went to her room. It was probably just my imagination but I realised that she would strongly disapprove of me misusing the photos and so I dropped that idea.

It was to be a difficult summer. I advised Barry to get Gareth Peirce as his solicitor, along with Michael Mansfield QC. I had been impressed by Peirce and Mansfield during the Birmingham Six appeal and thought that the *Dream Team* would see Barry free. A family friend got me Mrs Peirce's phone number and contact was established.

Mansfield was one of the top six defence lawyers in England, if not the best. The Daily Mail referred to him as a Champagne Socialist and he appeared to be hated by the Mail, some judges and lawyers. Jealously is said to be the reason for that. He represented the Price sisters who bombed the Old Bailey in 1973 destroying Mansfield's car in the process. 27 QCs became unavailable but he took on the case. The Guildford 4 and Birmingham Six appeals were amongst many other of his high profile cases. Fortunately Barry got Mansfield but he was adamant that he would keep solicitor Marilyn Etienne. I was horrified as I strongly felt that he needed a highly experienced lawyer such as Peirce, and I didn't know of Marilyn's track record. Michelle visited Barry along with Margaret to try and persuade him to change but it was not to be.

Acting on advice received I wrote to Marilyn asking that she resign from the case in Barry's best interests but she refused. I have good reason to believe that our phones were being tapped throughout that period, and that Barry was being 'got at' in Belmarsh. One evening prior to Margaret visiting Barry I advised her to borrow a mobile phone when going to the prison, get his permission to hire Mrs Peirce and phone her as soon as she left the visiting area. But when Margaret met Barry he was very agitated insisting that he did not want Peirce. I do know that a prison officer at some stage advised Barry that he was all right with the solicitor he had. It seemed to me that the powers that be did not want him to have Mrs Peirce, and influenced Barry accordingly.

Also, on May 26, the day after his arrest a number of inquiries were made to my phone company using my ex directory number and my customer account number, requesting an itemised account and a second line installed, neither of which I would need. It may just have been a reporter, like Jill Dando's 'utility stalker', but at the time I suspected police involvement. There was also interference with Margaret's phone by workmen who gave her the bizarre explanation that her phone number was being allocated to another customer.

On July 5 I wrote to Marilyn reluctantly accepting Barry's decision. From then on I would cooperate with Marilyn in any way I could.

The following Sunday I was feeling unwell due perhaps to the stress of recent events. On the Friday while driving a bus I had to swerve sharply and make an emergency stop to save the life of a young lady driver who made a near fatal mistake. The young lady did not even stop to see if I or any of my passengers were injured. Fortunately nobody was but I had been absolutely horrified firmly believing that I was about to kill the car driver which I would have had I not driven off the road. Before leaving for work on the Sunday I phoned Margaret who complained that she was also feeling unwell. On Monday I phoned again and her friend Annie answered saying that Margaret was quite ill. I contacted other London relatives who got her the help she required. I also informed Michelle who immediately returned to London. Margaret was unwell for the rest of the year which was a source of much concern for the family.

I felt that I needed to visit London but I was not very happy at the prospect. I was thinking of what happened to Giuseppe Conlon back in the mid '70s. As depicted in the film IN THE NAME OF THE FATHER Giuseppe's son Gerry had been arrested in what became known as the Guildford 4 case. Giuseppe then travelled over from Derry and he was also arrested. The innocent Giuseppe would die in prison. Before I left for London I got copies of my works roster of April 1999, one which I would take with me and the other I left with my diary of '99 in a safe place. I am not totally paranoid and had nothing to hide but I didn't know what to expect in London and I believe it pays to take sensible precautions.

Jill Dando

Jill Dando was regarded as the Face of BBC1, the Golden Girl, portrayed as the girl next door who every fellow over a certain age would like to date, and young girls would like to emulate. After her murder she was built up as a larger than life figure, angelic, a new Princess Diana for the nation and media to mourn. But Jill was a real person with feelings ambitions and maybe even some faults.

What is described as the definitive book on her life and death is ALL ABOUT JILL by David James Smith. With permission I have used the book as a reference for this brief synopsis of her life, though opinions expressed are my own.

Jill was born in 1961 to Jack and Jean Dando in Weston Super Mare, and was baptised into the Baptist Church. She was one of two children, Nigel being her older brother. She was lucky to survive childhood due to a heart defect but pioneering surgery saved her. She was very close to her mother. She followed in her father and brothers footsteps into a career in journalism and worked as a local reporter for a time before moving on to TV work. Her mother died in 1986.

In 1988 she moved to London to work for BBC Breakfast News, and later BBC News and the Holiday programme. Eventually she would co present BBC Crimewatch with Nick Ross.

She stayed for a time in her Cousin Judith Dando's small flat in Wimbledon. Judith was an ex army captain who had served in the Falklands before transferring for a time to the Ministry of Defence in London. Judith was about the same age as Jill and they had both grown up in the West Country. In 1988 Judith sold her flat and they bought a house in Heythorpe Street, Southfields. But sharing a residence had its little problems due to the very early hours that Jill's work entailed. She needed her sleep and late night music or entertainment in the house would disturb that. She is said to have briefly dated some of Judith's friends in her early days in London. Some of those people seem to have sailed a little close to the wind and one of them was jailed after killing a couple of people in a drink driving incident which is said to have horrified Jill. She apparently did not share what is described as the 'liberal lifestyle' of some of those around her and though she was known to occasionally smoke a cigarette she would never consider smoking a joint, as some around her might.

Judith Dando left London in 1990 for Serre Chevalier in France where she worked as a manager at the ski slopes. She lived among what are described as 'ski bums'. Jill visited her there from time to time but:

'did not much appreciate the steady flow of assorted ski bums and friends that Judith invited to stay at Heythorpe Street in her absence'

ALL ABOUT JILL

Possibly the biggest influence in her London life was her boss in Breakfast News, Bob Wheaton. Bob is reputed to have shaped Jill's career and transformed her from the frizzy haired West Country Girl to the polished TV presenter of the '90s. As part of her work she got to rub shoulders with royalty, such as the Duchess of Kent, Prince's Andrew and Edward, and the future Countess of Wessex. Andrew had met Judith Dando while they were serving in the Falkland's, where Andrew had flown helicopters during the 1982 war. Jill also became friends with Sir Cliff Richard and is said to have briefly harboured romantic notions for the *Bachelor Boy*.

One of the highlights of her time in Breakfast News was the military coup in the Soviet Union in 1991 when Mikhail Gorbachev was overthrown. The main presenter Nicholas Witchell was away and so Jill fronted the breaking news, guided by Bob Wheaton. Boris Yeltsin emerged as the hero of the fledgling Russian democracy which Gorbachev had pioneered in the Glasnost and Perestroika era of the 1980s, and the Soviet Union ended.

Bob has been described as a Svengali type figure, perhaps unfairly. Svengali is a character in the 1894 book Svengali and Trilby the Novel, written by the Englishman with a French name, George Du Maurier. In the novel Svengali gradually transformed his female victim Trilby through the abuse of hypnosis from an independent person into an obedient tool. He lived off the earnings she made as a successful singer created by him. When Svengali died Trilby could not survive without him and she also died.

Though Bob helped build Jill's career there is no suggestion that he profited from it or unfairly influenced her. It appears to have been a mutually beneficial relationship.

On at least one occasion Jill sported bruises and a black eye and wore dark glasses for a few days. The Sun did a report on 'Dando's shiners'. But it appears that she simply tripped and fell down the stairs at Heythorpe Street. It does seem fortunate that she did not suffer greater injuries after the fall, i.e. to her arms or neck.

She also formed other relationships. One was with Jan Knott, a travel firm director who she met in 1994 in Amman Jordan, while they were both working on a Holiday production which included travelling by Concorde. She once wrote to Jan ' . . . I didn't want to end such a magical trip on the doorstep . . . but in retrospect the doorstep was probably best.' Pursuing a relationship with Jan would be problematic as she was still with Bob though she wrote that the relationship with Bob was on the wane. But she and Bob would continue to be an item for another two years.

In 1994.Jill decided to sell her share in the Southfields house as she wanted her own place. She also loaned Bob Wheaton a sum of money to help him buy a house which he paid back to her estate after her death. Judith who was working in France was not in a position to buy Jill's share in the house and so it was sold. Due to the negative equity which hit the housing market in the early '90s the house fetched much less than what they paid for it. A few years later property prices had soared again and even after Jill's death Judith admitted to still feeling sick over it.

Jill moved into her new house, 29 Gowan Avenue, Fulham in early 1995. It appears that some friends advised her to live in a more secure residence with security but she wanted her own front door.

Jan stayed at Jill's house on a number of occasions. He would have liked a deeper relationship but fearing rejection he couldn't quite put his feelings into words. Jill wrote to him and seemed to leave the prospects open but she doubted if she was capable of '. . . DEEP love . . .'

In late October 1996 she had dinner with fellow Weston-man and author Jeffrey Archer. She mentioned that she would like to write a book sometime. Later she was the subject of the TV programme This Is Your Life. After the programme she had an argument with Bob over her having had dinner with Archer apparently without his wife Mary's knowledge. Bob feared the negative publicity for Jill if the tabloids got hold of that. Jill was due to meet Jan Knott for lunch next day but she made her excuses and cancelled. It appears that there were tensions as the relationship with Bob neared its end. Bob was approaching fifty and his career seems to have peaked while Jill's was still on the up. Jill's friends and family urged her to end things and move on.

Another man came briefly into her life, Simon Bassil, a game reserve ranger in his late twenties who she met on an African Safari again while working on Holiday. They fell in love under the African sky. The seven year relationship with Bob Wheaton finally fizzled out and they ended it amicably over a chat and a glass of champagne.

Simon moved from Africa to the UK where they continued their relationship. She described it as a 'very Lady Chatterley' relationship. It soon ended, but they remained friends.

Jill had lived a sheltered early life with her mother and appeared not to have broken out or let her hair down as many teenagers do until her mid thirties. Then she said she could have dinner with three different men in a week, and was 'quite skittish'. She may not have been as streetwise as one need's to be, and she seems to have mixed business with pleasure. Some of her relationships overlapped which may have exposed her to the usual jealousies most people experience; no matter how liberal minded they might claim to be. Some of her friends became somewhat concerned by the direction her life seemed to have taken.

In October 1997 her friend Jenny Hingham, a doctor, introduced her to Alan Farthing, a fellow doctor. He was a gynaecologist and also a Baptist who had recently separated from his wife of seven years Maria, who was a nurse. Jill invited him to her birthday party in November but he had a prior engagement. However Jan Knott and Simon Bassil did attend and it was their first time meeting each other. While Jill and Jan were sitting together on a sofa along with members of her family Simon is said to have come over and photographed them both which apparently caused Jan some confusion.

Later that day Jill invited Jan back to her Gowan Avenue house and he stayed there for the last time. They never met again as soon afterwards she settled into a steady relationship with Alan.

In an early 1998 edition of Hello Magazine she spoke exclusively from the Caribbean about romance and the new man in her life. Did she not hear of the curse of Hello, described by the UK Independent as a mysterious-hex on your romantic life the minute you appear in Hello?

Much of her private life appears to have been lived in the public eye, and photos were published at her front door or inside her house reclining on a sofa, feet in the air sporting bare feet and painted toenails. It was reported that she slept in a big brass bed wearing pyjamas and had a Teddy Bear. She and Crimewatch UK even featured in a 1998 episode of the TV series Goodnight Sweetheart though she did not actually appear in it.

Following a visit to Judith at Serre Chevalier in March 1998 a News of the World reporter informed Alan's estranged wife of his relationship with Jill. The paper then published photographs of Jill and Alan which were taken on the ski slopes. Alan did not welcome the publicity due to his profession as a gynaecologist. Unlike Jill, for Alan any publicity was bad publicity and Jill was quite upset believing that somebody had informed the press that she would be at Serre Chevalier.

A week later the Sunday papers reported that she had a stalker. He was retired civil servant John Hole from Kent. It appears that he first sent her a Valentines Day card and then graduated to waiting for her outside TV studios, phoning her and calling to her house. Mr Hole later said that he had only spoken to her once, in 1995. After a letter from him was pushed through her letterbox in 1998 she reported his interest to BBC security who said they would deal with him, but then somebody again tipped off the media which further upset Jill.

In December 1998 she told a solicitor friend Andrew Drew in Weston that she would love to meet some of his clients, maybe in prison. She might write a book when she was finished working as a TV presenter. Mr Drew did not take up her suggestion and it is unclear if she pursued her writing ambitions.

Jill and Alan became engaged in January 1999. It was covered by 6 pages of intimate engagement photos and a full interview in the March 5 edition of OK Magazine.

Maria Farthing was surprised when a tabloid reporter went and told her of the engagement. The wedding was set for September 25 and would be covered by Hello Magazine. Judith was to be a chief bridesmaid along with Jenny Hingham. Sir Cliff Richard and Gloria Hunniford were among the guests at the engagement party as was the then Sophie Rhys-Jones, later to be Countess of Wessex.

In the spring of 1999 Jill quit Holiday. She also lost out in a somewhat bitter competition to be the main presenter of BBC News at Six. She was now left with just Crimewatch and she looked around for other TV work. Her career had peaked but she could have presented for a couple more years until she reached the dreaded 40, the age when TV stations seem to think they should be replaced with younger models.

She put her house on the market as she was now staying with Alan in Chiswick, though she still kept her fax and work clothes in Gowan Avenue.

There was apparently some disquiet in her extended family due to her decision to get married in Fulham rather than in Weston. Judith and her mother Esme had words with her. It was felt that Weston no longer meant much to her. She had stopped staying there overnight; only making day trips and she said that she found Weston bleak. On her last two visits she did not visit her mother's grave as she usually would. It seems sadly ironic that though she did not wish to get married in Weston she would soon be taken back forever, to be buried alongside her mother.

On April 6 Jill made a controversial BBC appeal for the refugees of the Kosovo war. Two weeks later she was in Dublin working on her new TV series The Antiques Inspector.

On Saturday 24 Jill and Alan called to Gowan Avenue where she saw that there was a problem with her fax. In the evening they attended a British Legion charity ball. As part of his charity work Jeffery Archer auctioned a dance with Jill and an anonymous doctor successfully bid for it. At some stage in the evening as Jill and Alan left the dance floor they were approached by a mysterious young man whose detailed knowledge of Jill Alan found to be disturbing. The unidentified man is believed to be called Julian. It has never been established who he was. On Sunday they had a quiet day and watched the first episode of the Antiques Inspector.

Alan left for work early on Monday. Jill said that she would be a lady who lunches and at about 10.00 she left Chiswick for Gowan Avenue and a lunchtime fashion show at Hyde Park's Lanesborough Hotel. She would never reach the Lanesborough, meeting her death at the door of her beloved Fulham house, aged just 37.

Oxborough

When Jill left Alan's house she bought petrol and milk in a service station and spoke on the phone to one of her agents about a problem with her fax machine. She drove to Hammersmith and tried unsuccessfully to buy a printer cartridge. She then drove to Fulham where she bought two pieces of Dover Sole from Copes Fishmongers, apparently for an evening meal with Alan. She found an unusually convenient parking space in front of her Gowan Avenue house, zapped her car alarm, walked the two or three steps to her door, keys in hand where somebody pushed her to doorstep level and shot her once in the side of the head instantly killing her. The killer then left thoughtfully closing the gate. It is believed that two men saw the killer leaving the area, but they did not know what had just happened. Jeffrey Upfill-Brown who lived across the road watched a man jogging away and thinking that there was something suspicious made a mental note of the man. Richard Hughes who lived next door to Jill was in the process of having a shower and hearing Jill's car alarm, a scream and her gate clinking shut he looked out the window. He saw Mr Upfill-Brown across the road and got a sideways view of the face of a man who was departing the scene.

Shortly afterwards another neighbour Helen Doble saw Jill slumped at her doorstep and she ran to get help and dialled 999. She would later describe the scene as like 'Piccadilly Circus'* as frantic efforts were made to revive Jill, though it seemed obvious to Helen and two other ladies that she was already dead, her hands had gone blue and she did not appear to be breathing. Helen summoned help and hearing women's voices Richard Hughes came out and he saw Jill. There is some confusion as to whether one of the women asked Richard if the victim was Jill Dando. Richard thought one did but the woman denies that as she knew Jill by sight.

They removed her to the nearby Charing Cross Hospital and she was pronounced dead at about 13.00. Shortly after the body was removed from the crime scene the investigating officer DCI Hamish Campbell arrived. He would have preferred if the crime scene had been preserved. The police later tried to recreate the crime scene using a policewoman posing as the dead Jill. Unfortunately it is impossible to be sure where the killer came from. Was Jill followed to her door from the street, or did the killer wait behind the garden hedge, or even lay in wait inside the house? Was the intention to rob assault or kill her?

She did not appear to be robbed and there was no indication of a sexual assault. It is believed that the killer grabbed her right forearm which was bruised, and forced her down before shooting her.

Very little in the way of forensic evidence was found. The bullet which hit the door frame low down was recovered as was the cartridge case, a wet unidentified size 9 footprint and an antiques dealer's business card. The gate was removed by the police for forensic examination. It is unclear if it yielded anything. A lamp-post was removed down on the Fulham Palace Road where a running man was seen to grab it to steady himself.

Alan Farthing heard the news at his clinic in Saint Mary's Hospital. He was taken to the hospital by a policeman friend where he identified Jill's body. Jenny Hingham was also working at Saint Mary's at the time.

The murder occurred two months after the MACPHERSON Report into the racist killing of the black teenager Stephen Lawrence branded the Metropolitan Police institutionally racist, inefficient and incompetent.

Oxborough was a random name given to the Dando investigation which was headed by DCS Brian Edwards who had investigated the apparent murder of Susie Lamplugh, the Fulham Estate Agent who disappeared without trace after meeting a client in 1986. That case remains unsolved.

DCI Hamish Campbell was the chief investigation officer. Mr Campbell had at that time at least two unsolved murders on his books. He had investigated the rape and murder of a schoolgirl Katerina Koneva in 1997. Katerina was followed home from school and the killer is believed to have forced his way into her house when she opened the door. Her father surprised her killer when he returned home and the killer escaped through a window. Mr Campbell was troubled that despite having fingerprints of the killer the police were unable to trace him.

He had also investigated the disappearance of Gracia Morton in 1997. Gracia is believed to have been murdered by her husband.

Eventually Mr Campbell's persistence would solve both of those cases.

Operation Oxborough was a large operation which took 2,400 statements, checked 2000 potential suspects, 14,000 e-mails, 486 names which were in Jill's filofax, and traced 1200 cars. The murder squad was made up of 45 police officers.

Campbell made an early appeal to the public for information and the investigation was quickly snowed under. People reported seeing various things: blue Range Rovers, running men, sweating man at a bus stop, man jumping into the nearby river Thames, man chatting to a woman in the area about the circling police helicopters, (believed to be Barry George) man dumping a knife in the nearby Bishops Park, man or men seeing loitering near Dando's house and a man who visited a local disability advice centre and taxi office. (Barry George) All reports were fed into a Home Office computer known as HOLMES and were given priority ratings.

Those close to the victim had to be checked first as in most murder cases the victim knows the killer. Only 14% of female murder victims are killed by strangers, and almost half are killed by current or former partners or lovers. Alan Farthing was routinely questioned. His alibi was solid but police explored the financial angle. His recent divorce settlement was expensive so did he stand to gain from Jill's death? Jill's recently made will was made out in favour of Alan because they were jointly buying a house but the will would not become effective for another couple of weeks, so apart from her car he gained nothing financially from her death. As she died intestate her estate went to her father.

Then ex boyfriends, colleagues, criminals who might have been upset by Crimewatch, theories of a Serb or Mafia hitman, crime families and stalkers including the so called utility stalker all had to be checked.

Here is a list of some significant events following the murder.

April 27 1999. Police revealed that Jill Dando was shot.

April 29. BBC security stepped up after threats were made to the Director General.

May 30. E-Fit of suspect is released.

May 15. Barry Bulsara's (George) name was first brought to the attention of the police.

May 18. Crimewatch reconstruction.

May 21. Jill's funeral. Prince Edward's fiancée Sophie Rhys-Jones attended.

July 29. It was revealed that cartridge case had six crimp marks showing that the bullet was tampered with, possibly to reduce the noise of the gunshot.

September. A National Criminal Intelligence Service report named the Serbian Warlord Arkan as being behind Jill Dando's murder.

October 26. Cost of Operation Oxborough so far was put at £1,247,000.

December 5. Hamish Campbell became senior investigating officer following retirement of DCS Brian Edwards.

December 9. Police revealed Jill had a stalker.

January 16. Arkan was assassinated.

January 18 2000. It was revealed that a man posing as Jill's brother phoned her utility companies asking to get her bills changed into his name. The phone calls were made on the day after her engagement party. (Utility stalker)

February 24. DC John Gallagher assigned to trace Barry Bulsara. (George)

March 18. Campbell had 'gut feeling' that the murder was carried out by a lone man acting alone.

April 11. DC Gallagher questioned Barry Bulsara.

April 17 and 18. Police searched Bulsara's flat.

April 19. Second Crimewatch appeal. Police had mounting evidence that Jill was being stalked by an obsessed fan who secretly watched her house for weeks before shooting her.

Police reveal that some months before the murder a man phoned a woman called J Dando (not a relative of Jill) seeking information on Jill.

April 28. DC Gallagher took Barry's Cecil Gee coat from its forensically sealed parcel and opened it in a photographic studio where guns and ammunition had been.

May 2. Forensic scientist Robin Keely found single particle of firearms discharge residue on Barry's Cecil Gee coat.

May 25. Barry Bulsara (George) arrested.

May 28. Barry George (Bulsara) charged with murder.

Mr Campbell has been criticised due to the reliance placed on HOLMES. A case in point is a man who was reported to them just two days after the murder.

Staff at the local disability advice centre known as HAFAD reported a man who called on the day of the murder and who called back two days later speaking about it. They reported the man a number of times to the police, giving his name, address and date of birth. That man was Barry Bulsara, or George. Barry was known to the police due to his previous convictions. In 1992 they had routinely questioned him in relation to the Rachel Nickell murder case (which is now solved) and eliminated him from that inquiry. Now his name went into HOLMES as a low priority though the writer John McVicar claims that an unidentified policeman suggested in May 1999 that he should be checked out then. But he apparently remained hidden in HOLMES for a further ten months. His use of names may have resulted in the police not realising that Barry Bulsara was not also at different or overlapping times Barry George, Thomas Palmer, Steve Francis Majors and Paul Gadd all rolled into one.

Towards the end of 1999 the police did a review of the investigation which had seemed to be stalled. A psychological profile suggested the killer might be a loner, an obsessive or a stalker. Detectives spoke to experts in America about stalking, re-assessed their 2000 suspects and found that 140 of them had an unhealthy interest in Jill Dando.

In February the name Barry Bulsara surfaced again and DC John Gallagher was assigned to deal with him. Barry was Gallagher's 200th action and he had another 25 to do. It took Gallagher about six weeks to track Barry down. He dropped calling cards in Barry's letterbox asking him to make contact, but Barry claimed that he thought it was to do with a recent bicycle accident and that his solicitor was dealing with that. On April 11 Gallagher finally met him at a welfare benefits office.

As Barry is epileptic a responsible adult was needed during questioning and so Gallagher took him to his mother's house in East Acton. Barry told him he didn't know what time he left his flat on the day of the murder to go to HAFAD but agreed it was probably around midday. He didn't know what he was wearing but suggested a few combinations of clothes. Gallagher then drove Barry back to Fulham and had a quick look at the flat. On April 18 and 19 the police searched the flat.

The day after the search Hamish Campbell was interviewed on BBC Crimewatch by presenter Nick Ross who seemed intrigued by Hamish's theory of how the killer might be a loner, living alone, with an interest in guns or gun magazines that might have had an interest in Jill . . .

In early May it was reported that the police expected to make a breakthrough in the case. Meantime a squad of 50 police followed Barry around for two weeks and monitored his front door with a camera.

He was arrested at 06.30 on Thursday April 25, apparently by unarmed police officers. He answered all questions in the presence of his solicitor Marilyn Etienne until Sunday, when she advised him to exercise his right to silence. That was because the police had suddenly confronted him with forensic evidence which Etienne had not previously been made aware of. (That is in contrast to Sion

Jenkins, whose solicitor was apparently informed of the discovery of forensic evidence while Sion was being questioned in relation to the murder of his foster daughter Billie-Jo Jenkins) They claimed that a single particle of firearms discharge residue had been found in a pocket of Barry's Cecil Gee coat. He denied any knowledge of it. He was then charged with the murder of Jill Dando.

Barry was put in front of an I.D. line up but was not picked out even though Richard Hughes, one of the two men believed to have seen the killer viewed him. Acting on legal advice he refused to attend any more I.D. parades but the police set up a video parade and eventually one woman, Susan Mayes picked him out. She claimed to have seen him outside the Dando house at about 07.00 on the morning of the murder.

There was now forensic and eyewitness evidence and so enough to go to trial.

There were a number of failures in Operation Oxborough. A policeman was sacked from the team due to leaking of information to the media. Another policeman had an affair with a witness and was later accused of harassing her.

The mishandling of Barry's coat was a major failure and destroyed the integrity of the forensic evidence.

* In a March 16 2003 article published in Ireland on Sunday, a sister paper of the Mail on Sunday Helen Doble recalled:

'There was a great deal of blood. Her keys were in her left hand and I remember thinking it couldn't have been a robbery because her bag was open and her engagement ring was still on her finger. She was so obviously dead and it was so obviously a violent end that my instinct told me not to open the gate-not to touch anything.' She was shocked when the emergency services arrived by what followed. 'A police car and ambulance arrived and . . . more and more people trampled into Jill's garden and over what was, even to a lay person, very evidently a murder scene . . . her body was moved several times . . . it was like Piccadilly Circus. There was no photographs, no chalk circle-just chaos. I think they were panicked by the fact that they were dealing with a celebrity.' Helen accused the police of failing to act on her crucial information as the first person to come across Jill Dando and failing to provide her with any support in coping with her shocking experience.

Bow Street

I drove to London on July 30 and nervously entered Margaret's empty house after dark. It felt lonely in the house which was now empty except for Sheba, the cat and I recalled slightly happier times in the 1970s when the house teemed with life laughs and arguments.

I was a little concerned that the house might be raided during the night, and I locked all the doors and kept my clothes close at hand in case I had to get dressed in a hurry. Of course there was no raid and I felt a little silly later for fearing there might be.

Next day I went to Bow Street Magistrates Court, foolishly climbing all fourteen flights of stairs at Covent Garden station which shattered me. I was a little early so I popped over to the Aldwych for a cup of tea. When I entered the courtroom I was horrified to see that Barry had grown a beard, or goatee. I thought it made him look like a hard man. What the bloody hell is he playing at I wondered? 'Hey man, who is all those cameramen after then' I heard one young black man ask another. Barry was further remanded in custody and I slipped casually away unnoticed by the few photographers outside.

In the afternoon I visited Margaret in hospital. I contrasted how she looked compared to Barry and I felt a real anger towards him for all of this horror which had fallen on the family. He always wanted to be famous, and now he was, sort of, but for all the wrong reasons.

At home two weeks later I heard that there had just been another police raid, led by Detective John Gallagher. When a family friend arrived to feed Sheba the police were already in the back garden having gained access from next door. They demanded to be allowed into the house and said they would break the door down if necessary. Their metal detector bleeped causing some excitement and so they dug in the back garden and discovered the long dead dog 'Scamp's' aluminium feeding bowl.

How was Barry coping with prison life? We had virtually no information but it does seem that he was very stressed. In a letter from prisoner Razor Smith reproduced in John McVicar's book DEAD ON TIME Razor suggests that Barry might have been drugged with prescribed drugs. Apparently Razor met Barry in the prison hospital ward of Belmarsh in June. He described Barry as ordinary, not showing off in the role as a celebrity killer, quiet and softly spoken though shifty eyed. When asked why he was in prison he replied 'I don't know'. On being pressed he said 'the police say I done a killing'. 'And did you' asked Razor? 'No. I don't think so' replied Barry.

Barry thought he was on the drug Memoril which Razor says is prescribed for schizophrenics. Barry is not schizophrenic though Michelle did tell me in 2000 that the police did try to get a doctor to say he was, but the doctor refused.

Razor asked Barry if he liked guns and Barry replied 'what, guns and roses?' (A popular pop group) He denied liking real guns. Razor ended his letter:

'Perhaps George is a master criminal pulling the wool over everyone's eyes except the police. If so, he is also a brilliant actor and the police are rather more insightful than in my humble experience they normally are. Still, they may have discovered the smoking gun. The trial will tell. My overall impression was that he is very child-like and open to suggestion'. At the time of the interview, George was not a Cat A prisoner but that changed when he was moved out of the hospital.

John McVicar, DEAD ON TIME.

Jeffrey Archer mentions in his book A PRISON DIARY by FF8282 Barry's alleged clumsy participation in a prison sports day, falling over just 30 yards into a 100 yard race.

Barry can write but rarely sends a letter so though I would always write to him I only once got a letter from him. And that was simply a visiting order without any accompanying letter.

Barry George and me

'You're born, you know, the wrong names, wrong parents. I mean that happens. You call yourself what you want to call yourself. This is the land of the free.'

I first met Barry in 1964 when Margaret brought him from London to the family house in Limerick for a holiday. He was four and I was nine. I thought that he was very spoilt by Margaret but he was an only son. I think I bullied him a little but he may have got his own back. One day he asked me for a spoonful of sugar and instead being horrible I gave him some salt. Later as we played outside he threw an empty jam jar at me. As pain shot through my head I yelped in panic fearing that I was cut. Looking up I saw Barry staring wide eyed for a moment realising what he had just done, and then he bolted for the safety of the house. I chased after him wanting to kill him but my mother was close at hand and allowed him to escape into the house keeping me outside until I calmed down. I wasn't injured, just hopping mad.

I next met him in 1973, when I moved to London. Barry was now thirteen, his parent's marriage had ended and his father had left for a new family. He was attending Heathermount School 'for difficult boys', but would come home to his mother for holidays. His sister Susan was also living at home in East Acton. Barry and Susan were always bickering, as kids do. 'The terrible twins' we would call them, though Susan was two years older than Barry.

He was very quiet at first, withdrawn, but he slowly came out of his shell. I fixed up his old fashioned 'High Nellie' bicycle, and while the other kids in the street had modern choppers Barry could be seen doing quite impressive wheelies up and down Fitzneal Street. He liked my David Bowie records, and my Honda CB 250cc motorbike. 'Mike the bike' he would call me. He showed me around London, and he was quite streetwise. When we would go to the cinema he sometimes asked me to get him in via the fire escape, though I don't recall ever actually doing so. Being Irish in London at the height of the troubles it would not have been very wise to fall foul of the police. One day he 'borrowed' my Polaroid camera and used up all the film out around the streets. I did not develop the film but just threw it in the rubbish bin. It was the first time that I became aware of his interest in photography, an ongoing interest that would come back to haunt him.

His sister Michelle lived in Barnes with her father and his new partner Barbara, or Babs and their fierce little Chiwawa dog which kept Michelle's boyfriends at bay. It was a friendly lively household which I visited a few times; taking along some of my LP's which we would play. In late August 1973 Michelle borrowed my suitcase, went to Ireland for a holiday, liked it and stayed ever since.

Late one evening during that winter a man called to Margaret's to complain that Barry had just been involved in some antisocial incident. Margaret angrily told him to get lost, but I intervened, calmly explained to the man that Barry was away at the boarding school, many miles away. The man was then apologetic explaining that some of the other kids involved in the incident had given him Barry's name and address, blaming him.

Barry missed his father and Michelle, some say that he felt abandoned. One evening around midnight he still had not come home, and his mother asked me to make some checks. I went around to the public phone box and phoned his father in Barnes, but I was told that Barry was not there. I then phoned the police and explained the situation to them. Some time later Barry and his father arrived at the house, and there followed an interesting conversation between both parents at the front door as they complimented each other with regard to their parenting skills.

One morning in the summer of 1974 we were having an argument, quite nasty I suppose, as teenagers can be. As I was walking to the kitchen Barry seemed to come out of nowhere and floored me with a kick. He had been hiding, waiting in an alcove for me. I was winded, and Barry immediately bolted for the front door and was well away before I could catch him. He did not return to the house until late in the evening.

Sometime in the mid '70s his mother told me that he had recently had a fit. I was surprised as though I knew he was *different* I hadn't realised that he had epilepsy. I don't think anybody was aware of it until then.

He left school in 1976. He did not seem to have any career ambitions but he got a job for a short time at the BBC TV Centre as a messenger. One evening we were having a drink at the BBC Club, lager for me and coke for him. Suddenly his face lit up. 'I don't believe it, it's Freddie Mercury' he exclaimed wide eyed. 'Who is Freddie' I asked. He was amazed that I did not know who Freddie was but I had never heard of him up to that, though I was aware of the pop group Queen. I told him not to bother the group of long haired young men, who I understood to be from 'Queen'. But he just ignored me and went over to them and sat for a few minutes. They appeared to be very polite and he chatted with them for a short while. He beckoned at me to join them but I did not. Then one of them leaned over, tapped Barry on the shoulder and said something to him. Barry then came to me and said 'we have to get out of here'. He was in quite a panic and I told him to calm down, he hadn't done anything wrong. He said that they had told him that they were just having a quiet drink, but he insisted that he had to go. He really was in a panic, for no good reason I thought. We left.

His interest in Queen would also come back to haunt him.

He lived at home for a time after leaving school but could not get on with his stepdad Eddie who though being an honest hard worker found it difficult to tolerate young people. Barry managed to persuade the council to house him and everybody was happy again.

In 1977 I took a temporary job as a Security Guard, working with a collection of Australian and New Zealand backpackers and ex Rhodesian and South African soldiers at the Earls Court motor show. We worked in close cooperation with the police who would back us up if hostile members of the public ignored the instructions of us 'Little Hitler's'. One of my main tasks involved guarding Sir Donald Campbell's 400mph + Bluebird record setting car and the new Four Wheel Drive vehicles on which the gorgeous Woolworth girls would daintily sit to the song 'Who wants to be a millionaire', every 30 minutes. I was sick of that song. I would also check visitor's bags and briefcases with a sniffer device for detecting explosives etc. Barry thought it was hilarious that I, a 'Paddy just off the boat' was selected as one of the 'guards tasked to keep the royal fans in check when Princess Margaret performed the official opening ceremony. Looking back I also find it a little surprising but I guess the police would have checked us all out by then. I suspect I was selected more for my short neat haircut rather than for my security expertise but of course it was the Princesses personal bodyguard who provided the *real* security which at the time I thought was a bit over the top. But there was a very real threat of bombings or worse and we all took our jobs *very* seriously, even the scruffy looking lads. People's lives depended on us and the Rhodesian and South African ex-soldiers emphasised that, as did the police who we would sometimes have meals with. They were quite dangerous times, and we had to wear coats over our uniforms when going home. Less than two years later Prince Charles favourite Uncle Lord Mountbatten 'Dickie' was blown up by a bomb which had been planted during the dark night in his unguarded boat in Mullaghmore, Sligo. Two of his relatives and a local boy were also killed, while over to the east at Warrenpoint 18 Paratroopers were killed in an apparent revenge attack for the 1972 Bloody Sunday events. Prince Charles had been appointed Colonel in Chief of the Para's in 1977. The following day I saw that while Mountbatten's killing was quite understandably on the front page of a Red Top tabloid the 18 dead soldiers were relegated to the back page. Class distinction even in death, I thought.

One day in the late '70s Margaret was very annoyed with Barry. She told me that he had told her that in future he wanted to be called by another name, possibly Paul Gadd. Barry correctly explained that it was perfectly legal to change ones name. 'Well in this house you will always be Barry George whatever else you call yourself', she retorted. Over the years Barry would adopt different names, Steve Majors, Thomas Palmer, Barry Bulsara etc. It was a source of amusement to some of us and he got the nickname Glitter, as in Gary Glitter who was originally Paul Gadd. Barry was big into pop and movie stars and appears to have changed his name to emulate them. Gary Glitter, Cliff Richard and Freddie Mercury are just a few examples of celebrities who changed their names so it would seem quite ok for Barry to follow suit. He wanted to be famous also but within the family he was always known as Barry George or 'Glitter'.

Those name changes would come back to haunt him.

Barry had an interest in martial arts in the late seventies, and wore a white jumpsuit most of the time. I think that interest was sparked by the Kung Fu TV series, starring David Carradine. At one stage he boasted that he would smash something like seventy roof tiles with a karate chop. We did not believe him, but according to media reports a local west London paper did and published a story in which he claimed to be a champion. Of course he wasn't and he was soon exposed, but at the time I was totally unaware of that silly claim.

He also had an interest in being a stuntman, and claimed he would jump over four double deck buses on his roller skates. To my amazement many years later I saw on TV news footage that he did just that. He did tell us that at the time, but we did not take him seriously. I felt a bit mean over that as it took some nerve and though not a perfect leap he did what he set out to achieve, and nobody in the family said well done.

One day around 1980 a chain letter arrived for him. It warned of the usual murder death and destruction if he did not circulate it further. It quite spooked him, but Eddie and I advised him to ignore such rubbish and to chuck it in the bin. Some years later I found a chain letter in my work locker, but I did not read beyond the first line.

In the mid-1980s I had a nightmare in which a close family member, not Barry, was in prison for murder. It was simply unbelievable that the person in question could have done such an awful thing and it was the saddest bleakest feeling. I was very relieved to wake up and realise that it was not for real.

In the early 1980s I worked with the BBC and at first I feared that Barry might call in the hope of meeting Star's or Starlet's and so I kept that a secret from him. I was not involved in anything glamorous, working far behind the scenes, but I occasionally did a little security work at shows such as Sir Robin Day's Question Time, Top of the Pops, Wogan, Blankety Blank etc. My closest brush with fame was when working on 'Wogan' in the Shepherds Bush Theatre. A rude bald old man in the centre of the audience heckled Terry and made for the stage. I began moving down the side preparing to grab the old fellow when I noticed the stage manager laughing and I realised that it was just part of the show. The heckler was the excellent Warren Mitchell of Alf Garnett fame.

When Barry eventually found out where I worked the most he ever asked for was a copy of the Ariel, the BBC staff paper, or the Radio Times. He might have also asked for a ticket to Top of the Pops but those were like gold dust and I never got him one.

But that interest in the BBC would also come back to haunt him.

Various relatives of Barry and I had served in the armed forces of both our countries. I joined the Irish Army as a recruit in January 1972 but when basic training ended I exercised my option and got out 'on my ticket'. Barry also developed an interest in the army.

After the Princes Gate Iranian Embassy siege of 1980 he became interested in the SAS, and that grew during the Falklands war of 1982. He was then training with the Territorial Army. He called to visit me one evening at my place in Shepherds Bush, dressed in army gear and carrying a large kitbag. He told me that he had to report to barracks due to the war. I walked him to the bus stop which was next to my local pub, the Askew Arms. He wanted to come in with me but I lied and told him that it was full of mad Irish who would attack him because of his uniform. I was relieved when the bus came and he was gone. *Goodbye, Tommy Atkins.*

Later in 1982 we were at his sister Michelle's wedding in Cork. Barry had made his own way over on the car ferry. Susan was also at the wedding as was his mother and father. At the reception in Blackrock Castle I was less than impressed to find that I was seated with Barry, when the place was full of good looking young women. Cupid was absent at the planning. At one stage I had to get him outside as he was shaking and I feared he might throw a fit. Sometimes when he would visit my place in London he would be shaking quite a bit which I used to find quite unnerving. Fortunately at the wedding he was ok once he got some fresh air. Later he helped some of us to temporarily immobilise Michelle's husband's car for the 'going away' prank while others decorated it with shaving foam and tin cans tied to the rear bumper.

Late in the evening as I approached the bar for a drink I noticed an odd sight. Barry was on one side of the small bar facing a group of young men who I did not know. I overheard him say 'Who dares wins' and realised to my horror that he was talking about the SAS. I caught their attention and discreetly shook my head, and got him away from the bar. I was furious as I asked if he was a good swimmer. I then pointed down to the fast flowing river and warned him that he could end up in it if he continued to talk like that. Memories of the awful hunger strikes of 1981 were still fresh, and Barry could easily have passed for a real soldier with his height and short smart haircut. I warned the family to keep an eye on him for the rest of the evening. It was not the time or the place for such fantasy, he just did not realise the trouble silly talk could land him in. Many years later one of the young men who was at the bar sold a cock and bull story to the Irish Mirror claiming incorrectly to be Barry's brother in law.

Barry was not very practical minded or dexterous. If the back garden at Margaret's house needed tidying or a small electrical fault needed fixing I would do it, while Barry would remain inside watching TV. Probably as a result of his lack of dexterity he did not fit in very well with the TA. In 2002 his friend Robert Charig revealed on a Cutting Edge TV programme that other recruits would not pair off with Barry during exercises and so Robert would sometimes go along to train with him.

Around the end of 1982 he told me that he was leaving the TA as he had failed their 'Cadre' as he described it. He then announced that he would be joining the part time SAS which made me laugh. 'You fail the TA and so the SAS will now take you', I mocked. He had a fearsome looking SAS knife, an ornament which might just about cut butter.

Again that military interest would come back to haunt him.

One evening while visiting me he developed abdominal pains which worried him. I drove him to the nearby Hammersmith Hospital where a motherly looking nurse examined him. 'Perhaps I am pregnant' he joked causing her to laugh and say 'you would be making medical history'. His concern about the pain appeared to quickly evaporate, but I did notice over time a tendency in him to be a bit of a hypochondriac.

Unfortunately he had a side to him which I had not been very aware of. I always thought of him as a more or less harmless character who was a bit of a fantasist but that was not quite the case. In early '83 his mother told me that he was in prison on remand. At his trial in the Old Bailey he pleaded guilty to a serious offence in February 1982 and got thirty months in prison. As Barry is once again trying to get on with his life I have decided not to go into the details which have received much press coverage but I do recall reading in a newspaper at the time that he initially denied it but that the detective tripped him up by asking him if he spoke any German. Barry replied 'Ich Verstain', (I understand). It appears that he used the same expression to the unfortunate victim who was a student studying German. So it would seem that a clever detective had no trouble in tripping him up and getting to the truth.

He served his time in Wormwood Scrubbs, Brixton and Grendon Underwood prisons. I visited him a couple of times along with his mother and Eddie. He was free again by Christmas 1984 and he seemed to settle down after that. He never spoke to me about the crime and I never asked but I read her own account in 2001 following his conviction for Jill Dando's murder, and again in 2008 when she wrote that she doubted if Barry was a killer.

Barry had a 125cc motorbike in the summer of 1986 which I thought was surprising given his epilepsy. It was a nice 'bike and I had a spin on it. But one day a woman motorist pulled out in front of him and the 'bike was wrecked. A taxi driver witnessed the accident and he wrote in a witness statement that 'she didn't give the poor fellow a chance'. I don't think that he was seriously injured in the accident, just cuts and bruises and possibly a leg injury. After that he wisely decided to give up motorbikes and bought a mountain-bike.

It appears that in the late 80's he tried unsuccessfully to join a pistol shooting club in Kensington. I don't recall him ever speaking to me about an interest in guns, and that news came as a surprise to me when I read about it years later. He would talk about other interests, like photography, stunts, martial arts etc but I was not aware of any interest in guns. But I suppose somebody fixated with the SAS would also have had to have an interest in guns, which would also come back to haunt him.

He got married in 1989. I was not invited to that and I never met his wife, Itsuko Toide, a Japanese language student. He never spoke to me about her and I never asked. The marriage was short lived and there have been reports of domestic violence. At the time I assumed that the marriage was one of convenience and I was surprised to read many years later that they had actually lived together. Itsuko revealed in 2001 that she had married him so as to be able to stay in the UK, and she also claimed that he beat her.

Itsuko refused to allow herself to be used in the case against Barry.

Shortly before I left London in 1990 I remarked to Eddie that Barry seemed to have settled down and kept out of trouble. Eddie then told me how when he was freed in 1984 he had taken him to one side, out of earshot of Margaret and warned him to behave himself in future as he would now be a marked man and could expect the police to come knocking from time to time. 'He seems to have learned his lesson', Eddie said.

I met him just a couple of times in the 1990s and I assumed that he was just drifting harmlessly through life as most of us do. Towards the end of her life my mother often asked me where he was living, who was looking after him? I thought that as with most of my relatives he would eventually disappear from our everyday lives. I could never have guessed what lay ahead.

Committal

2000

In June a number a reporters contacted me. One was Amanda Perthen who was then working for the Sunday People. Though nervous of dogs she braved Shannon's barking and came to my back door while a man remained outside in a car. I invited her inside and we chatted about Barry. She said that they wanted to run a storyline saying 'He is innocent' to reflect public opinion, but nothing ever came of it. One day over the phone she told me that 'a copper' told her that due to advances in forensic testing DNA could now be detected from a spent bullet, left by acid in the sweat of the person who handled it.

Another reporter who contacted me was Margaret Renn, a freelance journalist who once worked for the BBCs Rough Justice programme. Margaret would be very helpful in the dark year's ahead.

I began sending Barry regular mail to try to keep him in touch with the real world. I never once got a reply but that did not bother me. In late August it was confirmed that Michael Mansfield QC would be on the defence team, so things were looking a little positive. At least now Barry would have a fighting chance.

In early September Barry's aunt Betty and his local Baptist church minister the Reverent John Hale were approved as visitors.

On October 10 I drove to London for the committal hearing which began the next day. Betty, Michelle and I went together to Bow Street Magistrate's Court. I carried a small black travel bag with some clothes and a disposable razor for Barry to use if he was released. He was late arriving in court due to traffic delays caused by Reggie Kray's funeral. We met Mike Fuller of the Metropolitan Police who helped us get a seat. He was very polite to us and Betty seemed to strike up a friendly rapport with him as he seemed very open and approachable.

Commander Fuller was head of the West Serious Crime Group and had overseen the investigations of high profile cases such as Suzy Lamplugh, the Notting Hill Carnival murders of 2000 and Jill Dando. He would later be promoted to Assistant Chief Constable of the Met, Chief Constable of Kent, and was tipped to replace Sir Ian Blair as Chief Constable of the Met in 2008.

Jonathan Laidlaw made the case for the Crown with Marilyn Etienne and Michael Mansfield for the defence. Laidlaw told the hearing how Barry had gone to HAFAD and Traffic Cabs on the day of the murder and returned to both premises two days later asking that they recall his earlier visit. He described how firearms residue was found in Barry's coat, and how a witness had identified Barry at the scene of the crime early in the morning.

Naively at lunch time we went out for tea. We were mobbed by cameramen and Betty injured her ankle in the crush, while I ended up *accidentally* bumping against one of them. It was an unpleasant experience and we were all shaken by it. It was just our first taste of what was to come. To avoid a repeat the police drove us from the court to a tube station after the court ended.

On Thursday 12 Barry was committed for trial, despite Mansfield's best efforts. He was worried about it going to a jury, and said he would try to get the trial judge to stop it. I could not believe anyone could be tried on the little evidence that was presented. Up to that point I thought that the police might have had some damming piece of evidence up their sleeves. The prosecuting barrister Jonathan Laidlaw had argued successfully that there was enough evidence for a jury which was properly directed to convict. I briefly met Margaret Renn at the court and we agreed to meet again at a later stage.

In the evening I visited Margaret in hospital, where I broke the news that Barry would have to stand trial. Michelle later arrived having accompanied Betty to her home. Unfortunately Betty would not attend any more court hearings. I never met her again though she would later confirm to the JfB campaign that she continued to believe that Barry was innocent. I am aware that Betty may have spoken to the police in support of Barry. It appears that Barry was told that she could be used against him and so he had no further contact with her. I believe she was a great loss in the years which followed.

On Friday 13 I visited the BBCs Rough Justice office meeting team members Tanya and Louise. They were interested in the case as I had contacted them earlier and had hoped we could work with them. They seemed keen but others in the family were not and so that idea floundered. I was disappointed as Rough Justice had said they would follow up on cases which they covered rather than making one off programmes. I began to realise then that I was on a slightly different track to others and I wondered did we all fully appreciate the gravity of Barry's predicament. The priority should be doing all we could to get him cleared of the charges as he was facing the rest of his natural life behind bars if he was convicted. Though of course we all shared that aspiration I lacked confidence that faith and faith in the British justice system alone would see us through and so I wanted to utilise the media. But Rough Justice was now effectively lost and it would be many years before I would get such a good opportunity again.

I was still trying to get Home Office approval to visit Barry but they appeared to be dragging their feet. I was in touch with the Irish Department of Foreign Affairs, and HMP Belmarsh. Belmarsh informed me that Scotland Yard were handling my application for approval. They obviously were in no hurry to approve me and it was an ongoing struggle against obstinate officialdom.

Celebrity

2000-'01

'Alastair Campbell, Tony Blair's official spokesman, was quizzed by detectives over the murder of TV golden girl Jill Dando, police sources confirmed last night. Mr Campbell met Scotland Yard officers so that they could eliminate him from their inquiries.

He was interviewed after a British newspaper wrongly claimed he had joked about being a former lover of Miss Dando at a lunch party.

Mr Campbell was never seriously suspected of gunning down Miss Dando at her south London home in April 1999, the paper says. But officers felt obliged to interview him after spotting a letter to the paper strongly denying the diary claim'.

The Irish Sunday Independent carried that report on page 10 of their November 12 edition. Sky News text also reported the story at 00.07 on the 12th, and attributed the report to the Sunday Times.

The story first surfaced in September 1999 in Matthew Norman's Guardian Diary. Mr Campbell immediately complained to the editor and apologies were offered.

I returned to London for the preliminary hearing at the Old Bailey on November 24. Margaret was home from hospital now. I entered court via the Newgate entrance, following a few American visitors to the public gallery. I overheard one say 'Gee, all those cameras, there must be some celebrity here today'.

There appeared to be some confusion as the hearing started. Barry was late arriving and when he did nothing much seemed to be happening. Then Mansfield approached the dock and spoke quietly with Barry. Mansfield then nodded to the judge and the proceedings began. It was a short hearing and a provisional date for the trial was set, February 26. Later Michelle told me that Mansfield had thought that Barry was going to sack him hence the confusion in court. That was something that we would all have to come to terms with in the years which followed.

I met Margaret Renn later in the fish and chip shop in East Acton. She said that Barry would need all the family support he could get. She asked me if I would give her an interview, and I said probably not as I was unpopular enough with some of my family.

The following day I went with Barry's mother to Belmarsh prison. It was her first visit since the early summer when she was taken ill. She discovered that he was being punished due to being taken ill after the court case and giving a prison officer a back answer. He got two weeks solitary as a result, and the visit was cut to less than an hour.

I still was not approved as a visitor despite sending in the forms and photographs as required. It looked as if they were stalling, and I was getting nowhere until one day Margaret Renn phoned the prison and asked in her best BBC accent why I was not approved. And so I was finally approved.

I visited Barry in December, seven months after I last met him. I took my passport, letters of approval, and three photos which were stamped by my local Garda Sergeant to confirm they were of me. My right hand was stamped with a yellow mark, and I had to look into a camera which scanned and memorised my features. I then had to put my hand into a palm scanner, three times. We had tea in the visitor centre, and I deposited the contents of my pockets in a personal locker, keeping a hankie and a few coins for the vending machine. We then joined the queue at the main entrance, where I gave my shoes and jacket for to be x-rayed. My hand was checked again, I was frisked, opened my mouth so they could see if I had anything illegal in it, and lifted my feet so they could check my soles. We then went into the main visitor area where we were separated from the other visitors. Barry was classified as Category 'A', so we had to go in a prison van to the Cat 'A' area. More checks followed, and finally we were allowed to meet him.

I was pleased to see the beard was gone. He had a silly looking red bib around his neck to signify Cat 'A'. We shook hands, mainly for the benefit of the cameras and prison officers who watched our every move.

We quietly discussed his defence team, but he would not discuss the case. He did indicate that he was not the killer, and denied having a dislike of the BBC. He reminded me that I knew that he would have liked to go back to work with them again.

We got drinks from the vending machine and chatted for a while. We were interrupted a couple of times by prison officers who queried my right to visit.

Barry was pleased with the visit, and asked me if I would be a character witness for him, as I had worked for the BBC. I agreed, if required.

He was a little concerned about me meeting Margaret Renn, but agreed it was ok if I thought she could be trusted. I assured him she could be. The visit ended.

At Christmas I encouraged some people to send Christmas cards and he was very pleased to get them. My reason for that was to demonstrate to the powers that be that he was not on his own.

In January the Sunday People published a 'Randy Cop' story. Apparently a policeman on the case had an affair with one of the key witnesses, a married woman.

Barry entered a not guilty plea on Thursday 11. Michael Mansfield QC advised us that some family should attend the trial. Unfortunately it appeared that no family from the UK would be attending so it would be up to me and Michelle. Marilyn Etienne informed me that I could be called as a character witness. Family tensions were running high in the run up to the trial and a number of tense letters were exchanged between me and other members. Fortunately we managed to remain cordial though I became aware that I was held in contempt by some who thought I should not be involved. For me that became the biggest hurdle over the coming years as I came to believe that I was in a no win situation, but I was not going to walk away unless Barry asked me to.

I visited him again on February 9 and it was quite a pleasant visit in as far as prison visits go. We discussed the upcoming trial and I gave him some advice. He said he would like if I could be in court throughout the trial but I had to explain that I could only be there part of the time due to my work commitments.

I promised to get some newspapers delivered to him and when I got home I organised that through a Belmarsh newsagent, THE FRONT PAGE.

I also sent him a Good Luck card which many of the family signed. I had been advised that it was important to demonstrate our support for him.

On February 19 at 00.10 Sky News advertised wall to wall cover of the trial. They continued to run the ad for the rest of the week. It looked as if they were billing it as the next OJ Simpson type trial.

Trial

POISE THE CAUSE IN JUSTICE EQUAL SCALES.

Sign over Court No 1

(William Shakespeare)

The trial initially commenced on Monday February 26 2001. Michelle and I entered The Old Bailey unnoticed. We were allowed into the main body of Court Number One rather than the public gallery which is the usual. We were allocated a bench which nobody else was allowed to occupy. I was amazed to see all the boxes of files relating to the case, about two hundred I estimated.

The Dando camp and Alan Farthing were sat behind us, and some of the press and police were behind them. Forward to our right were the Prosecution lawyers. A little to our left were the defence and Barry on our left in the famous dock which had been used in the trials of John Christie of 10 Rillington Place fame and former armed robber now journalist John McVicar. The jury would sit on the far left facing the lawyers and next to the witness stand. The stand has a little roof, as the original Old Bailey did not have a roof and everybody except the witness giving evidence were exposed to the elements.

The trial judge was Mr Justice Gage with Senior Treasury Counsel Orlando Pownall for the Crown along with Jonathan Laidlaw. Michael Mansfield QC and Maryam Syed instructed by solicitor Marilyn Etienne for the defence.

A general outline of the case was given, and there was some legal argument. The Crown's skeleton case was that Barry George was seen hanging around Jill Dando's Gowan Avenue house on the morning of her murder. That he shot her shortly after 11.30 and then in order to remove the gun and any blood evidence he returned to his home a mere 600 yards away. He then changed his clothes and made his way to HAFAD, stopping to talk to a woman Julia Moorhouse, at about 12.30. He also made a mobile phone call to his service provider at 12.32. It was claimed that a blurred yellow figure caught on CCTV at 12.48 was Barry as he passed Fulham football ground on the way to the HAFAD disability advice centre, where he stopped briefly before going on to the Traffic Cars minicab office arriving there at about 13.00. He then managed to get a free cab ride at 13.15. It was claimed that Barry's visits to HAFAD and Traffic Cars was to seek sanctuary and to create a false alibi.

It was also claimed that when questioned he lied to police about his movements on the morning of the murder, that a witness identified him in Gowan Avenue prior to the murder, and that firearms discharge residue (FDR) was found in an inside pocket of a coat which he said he could have been wearing on the day of the murder.

The four main points on which the prosecution based its case were the alleged false alibi, lies told to police during questioning, the FDR, and witness identification.

The defence claimed that nobody saw Barry hanging around Gowan Avenue in the half hour prior to the murder. No one identified him at the scene of the crime at the time of the crime. He could not have done the crime as he would not have had time to go home and change his clothes, having committed the crime at 11.30 and be at HAFAD at 11.50 or 12 noon. He did not possess a gun and had no access to weapons. His flat was filthy and there was no sign of any recent cleaning, for example no areas of the carpet seemed to have been cleaned.

On Tuesday Mr Justice Gage lifted the ban on photos of Barry being published. Immediately there was a mad dash from the court as the reporters rushed to phone their editors. Barry's photo was on the lunchtime TV news. In the evening I was nearly knocked over by the cameramen. One had a camera almost up my nose as I walked away from the Old Bailey. Then they all dropped back except for one who ran ahead of me and knelt as if to take a still photograph. Suddenly he sprang up and shoulder charged me as he passed. Fortunately he hit me too hard to allow me to react, as Michelle said his fellow cameramen were lined up to capture any response from me. I believe it was the photographer's revenge for me 'bumping' the cameraman at Barry's committal. If so they failed to get a reaction.

As we approached Saint Paul's tube station we saw Barry's 'mug-shot' on the front of the Evening Standard. Inside he was shown in handcuffs. Carlton TV showed a grotesque artists impression of him and his mother was very upset by it.

On Wednesday the tabloids published every lurid photo of Barry which they could get their hands on. Barry was said to have felt personally devastated and Mansfield went absolutely ballistic. The case now had an aura of guilt about it he claimed. Pownall expressed his regrets, and Gage struggled to justify his decision to allow publication. Eventually he re-imposed a partial ban, and the defence team in consultation with Michelle and I agreed a single photo which could be used in future. Mansfield accused either the police or the prison authorities of having released the official mug-shot, and he challenged them to deny that. They never did. Mansfield then argued that a fair trial had been compromised, and that unsure witnesses could be influenced by the photos.

On Thursday Gage ruled that the trial could go ahead. The court was then cleared for legal argument until 14.00, and at 14.02 it was again cleared until 16.00. Then Mansfield, 'with a heavy heart' asked Gage to adjourn the trial. Gage agreed, and strict reporting restrictions were imposed.

On Saturday March 3 Margaret, Michelle and I visited Barry at Belmarsh. I again got hassle from prison officers over my identity photos. I put that down to harassment as I had no problem in February. To make a bad visit worse Barry accused me of sending him a 'sensitive' letter, but I had actually sent it to his solicitor. In time we would get used to his complaints and threats of court actions against us and others who were trying to help him.

I drove home on Sunday, departing London at about 08.00. I discovered later that at approx 08.30 a car bomb had exploded outside the BBC TV centre. I had no wages to get when I got home as I had been on unpaid leave, but the taxman generously gave me a small refund.

On April 20 I wrote a letter to Paddy Hill, one of the Birmingham Six, who had formed a prisoner support group called MOJO. I had heard him being interviewed on RTE Radio and I was quite impressed. I wrote that I feared that Barry would be 'stitched up' and requested the help of MOJO.

Legal argument began on Saint George's day, April 23. The jury was soon sworn in, seven women and five men. A good mix, we thought. Michelle was there alone, I would go later. The actual trial began on Friday May 4. I was surprised when I saw it reported on Sky News as there had been a virtual news blackout up to then, and the papers were full of it on Saturday. On Sunday I again drove to London. Monday was a public holiday and I went to the court on Tuesday.

Prosecution.

Pownall described Jill Dando's background, her TV career and marriage plans. He ran through her last morning and told the jury that the killer was Barry George and no other. He discounted a hit-man theory as there was no evidence that she was followed from Chiswick, and nobody except her fiancé and her agent could have known that she would be visiting her house on that day. She no longer lived there, the house was for sale. Therefore it was more likely that it was the defendant who lived nearby, who had been observed hanging around Jill's house. He had a dislike for the BBC and had an obsession with celebrities, guns and the SAS.

A couple of BBC female employees gave evidence, and they said that Jill Dando was not threatened by anyone, but then it was revealed that she had been pestered by a stalker, Mr Hole from Kent. Jill's previous relationships were also referred to.

A statement was read from Alan Farthing who didn't speak, despite being in court. His divorce and his ex wife Maria was mentioned. The mysterious Julian from the British Legion Ball was also referred to.

BBC employee Sophia Wellington recounted how a man who could have been Barry spoke to her outside the BBC Centre in White City and said that he did not like the way the BBC treated Freddie Mercury's family after he died.

Alison Hoad described a 1997 visit to Fulham, taking her young daughter for an audition. A man who could have been Barry spoke to her and guided her to the audition venue. At one stage he pointed in the general direction of Gowan Avenue and said that a 'Special Lady' known to him lived there. Electoral checks showed that Jill Dando was the only celebrity living in that area.

Susan Coombe lived at an address which Barry also lived at in 1985. She described how he had replica guns which he showed to people. But she also said that there was a silver gun which he kept concealed in a shoebox. She claimed that he admitted to her that he followed women to see if they were single. Susan also confirmed that the photo of the man posing with the gun and gasmask was taken inside Barry's home.

A number of witnesses then gave details of a man seen in the vicinity of Gowan Avenue, and some also referred to sightings of a blue Range Rover which was seen in the area.

Witness Susan Mayes had picked out Barry at a video I.D. parade. She claimed to have seen him at 07.00 on the morning of the murder, standing by a double parked car. She said 'I saw the defendant; he was standing by a car'. Mansfield asked her why she used the word defendant. Eyes shining she defiantly retorted 'I am looking at him now'.

Under cross examination Mansfield then exposed an inaccuracy in her evidence. In court she described the man she had seen as thuggish, with hair down over his collar. But a policeman recorded her description of him on the day of the murder as having 'A short smart haircut'. She could not explain the discrepancy. (Pownall later claimed that it may have been the policeman who wrote down her description incorrectly)

Postman Terry Griffith saw a man at about 10.00 who he thought seemed to be acting suspiciously. He thought he might be going to 'nick' something from his barrow. As he had witnessed something Terry was taken off his round for six weeks. Then on his first day back a man approached him talking about Jill Dando and saying he had just seen somebody who might be her killer. Terry dismissed the man as a nutter. At the I.D. parade Terry failed to identify the man he first saw, but he picked Barry George as the second.

Terry Belinda Normanton was described by Pownall as suffering from a mental condition which could cause her to take time to match events and times. She was on her way to an embroidery class and claimed to be fairly sure that she saw a man like Barry with a mobile phone to his ear, near to the crime scene at about 10.00. But it was a year after the murder before she approached police. She said that she would have picked out the man portrayed in the E-Fit if he had been on the ID parade.

Stella de Rosnay described looking out the window of her son Alexis's Gowan Avenue house and seeing a man crossing the road who reminded her of Alexis, a city worker.

Stella's daughter-in-law Charlotte de Rosnay also saw the man who she described as smartly dressed but not 'city smart', more like an estate agent who had a 'Desperate Dan' look.

Richard Hughes worked from home trading in Far East stocks and shares using his home computer. He lived in the house next to Jill Dando's. He was upstairs about to take a shower when he heard Jill's car alarm zap and her footsteps as she walked to her door. He described her scream which he likened to somebody being surprised by someone they knew, rather than a cry of alarm. He then heard Jill's gate clink shut and he looked out the window to see a man calmly leaving. He got a look at the side of the mans face. The man was holding something in his hand, maybe a mobile phone, or it could have been a gun. Richard finished his shower and shortly afterwards hearing women's voices he went downstairs and saw Jill slumped at her doorstep. Richard did not identify anybody at the live I.D. parade.

Jeffrey Upfill-Brown described how he came out of his house across the road from Jill's and saw a man jogging away. Jeffrey was immediately suspicious and made a mental record of everything he could about the man. Jeffrey thought the man appeared to be wearing a wig. He had a look at his face as he looked back. He estimated the distance from the man at that stage was about the length of a cricket pitch. There followed an amusing conversation between Mr Justice Gage and the lawyers about the distance of a cricket pitch. It was agreed that it was about the distance between the judge's benches and the back of the courtroom. As Jeffrey was answering a question relating to his description of the man he nearly went further saying . . . 'actually I thought he' . . . Mr Justice Gage nearly jumped out of his chair leaning forward saying 'stop, you must only answer the question you are asked'. 'I'm so sorry' Jeffrey replied and Gage said it was all right but to remember to only answer the specific question asked. Mr Upfill-Brown did not identify anyone at the video I.D. parade.

Helen Doble described how she knew Jill Dando and would sometimes chat with her in the street or at the shop. She was on her way to have some photocopying done and noticed Jill's car. Hoping for a chat she looked to Jill's door as she passed and then everything changed. Jill was slumped in a pool of blood at her doorstep. It appeared obvious to Helen that Jill was dead so she dialled 999 and then ran to the doctor's surgery nearby for help. The doctor had gone out but a receptionist went to Jill's gate with Helen where they waited for the emergency services. Helen was tearful when giving her evidence and it was harrowing listening to the account of her dreadful discovery.

The man seen by witnesses was described as Mediterranean in appearance, dark haired with heavy eyebrows, late 30s or early 40s, approx five foot ten, stocky. There were variations in descriptions of height and skin but on the face of it there appeared to be a general consensus.

I became very uneasy as I felt that the descriptions of the man described could have fitted Barry.

On Thursday morning the court visited Fulham, and Mr Mansfield cut quite a dash on his blue mountain bike. The police did not recognise him and he was forced to wave frantically at Mr Justice Gage so as to be allowed entry to Gowan Avenue. The press loved it. Barry was forced to stay in the prison van in the sweltering heat, but at least they opened the doors.

On Friday he was ill allegedly as a result of mistreatment by prison officers in the courts holding room. That caused long delays, to the frustration of Mr Justice Gage, who wanted to move things along. As Pownall was leaving the room during the lengthy delay he passed a private remark 'matron is with the beleaguered'. Michelle was furious and I had to persuade her not to challenge Pownall. I was afraid we might be forced up into the public gallery if there was a scene, and the press would have loved it. But I can appreciate her anger at the pompous comment. Doctor Susan Young was surprised at Barry's apparent mistreatment.

On Saturday Michelle and I went to Belmarsh, but I could not go in for an open visit as I failed to pass the sniffer dog test. I wasn't carrying any drugs or explosives or planning a Rambo style breakout but I was treated very impersonally. I like dogs and the dog seemed to like me as it jumped up at me three times. I think the handler was a little surprised as he pulled the dog back. I was then offered a closed visit where we would have a glass screen between us. Suspecting a fit up I walked out in disgust and in so doing allowed Michelle to have an open visit. The lady in the tea bar thought that maybe there was something on the seat of a bus or train which I might have come into contact with. It was an odd experience. I never again felt at ease with the sniffer dogs even though I never failed the test again.

(Incidentally, during a Libyan terrorist threat in 1986 a sniffer dog detected something in my car boot as I was about to board a car ferry to Holland. After about an hour of incredibly thorough searching the amused police discovered the evil substance, a forgotten bag of pongy home made Scottish toffee)

For the rest of May I followed the case on the news and in phone calls to Michelle who attended court every day. Barry was ill at times, suffering various ailments including apparent blindness which caused amusement amongst the press reporters who believed that he was faking. I found it hard to believe also until some years later when I experienced a nasty migraine attack which gave me an incredible fright thinking I was going blind. So perhaps his attack was genuine brought on by stress.

Forensics

Barry was portrayed as a man who was familiar with firearms. He had been with the Territorial Army, had attempted to join a gun-club, and he had written details of handguns including a Bruni in his flat. The police had found advertisements in his flat for deactivated weapons showing where they could be bought but there was no evidence that he had the tools or skills to alter guns. A photograph of him wearing a gasmask and holding a handgun, finger on trigger was found by police. There was a break in the gun exposing a spring. That was said to show that he had an interest in altering guns. Barry denied during police questioning that it was him in the photograph, and claimed the gun; a blank firing replica was stolen by his friend David Dobbins.

In evidence David Dobbins described an incident where Barry discharged a blank firing pistol at David's mother's house, frightening him. David admitted that following his frightening experience he chatted with Barry, his friend, for about an hour.

When searching Barry's flat on April 17-2000 Police Constable Cain had found a coat and handed it to Detective Constable Isaacs who sealed it in an exhibits bag and it was sent to a police station. Both officers gave evidence of the precautions they had taken in relation to the surgical gloves and clothing worn by them.

On April 24 the coat was taken to Amelia Street Police Photographic Studio where it was removed from the sealed bag and photographed.

On May 2 it was taken to the Forensic Science Laboratory. There Mr Robin Keeley, a Senior Forensic Officer specialising in FDR examined the coat. In an inside pocket he found a single particle of firearms discharge residue, 11.5 microns in size. Two FDR particles which matched each other had also been found on Jill Dando's hair and raincoat. Keeley compared those particles with the one found in Barry's coat and they matched. Tests were carried out to exclude other sources for the particle.

In evidence Keeley said that the particle could have come from the ammunition which had killed Jill Dando or from similar ammunition. The residue would remain in a pocket indefinitely, unless the garment was disturbed. The residue would not decay evaporate or dissolve.

He was asked if it was significant that only one particle was found. He replied that there was no significance; it just meant that firearms residue was present. It would identify where it came from but not how it got there.

Our faith in Mansfield appeared to be justified, as he picked apart the scant forensic evidence and exposed the shortcomings of the police.

He asked Keeley to describe exactly how a coat including the inside pocket could be tested for particles. The single particle took up about three days of court time and was fiercely contested by both sides. It was revealed that it did not fully match the residue which was found in Jill Dando's hair, it lacked antimony, one of the four elements in the particles found on her.

Mansfield argued that the particle could have got in the pocket due to innocent contamination.

He grilled the police over their procedures for forensic testing. The POLSA police team which searched Barry's flat when the Cecil Gee coat was removed were not tested beforehand for contamination. They changed into their search clothes in police stations and in the police van. The van was not tested beforehand either. The police wore ordinary police blues rather than white forensic suits, gloves and overshoes. Therefore he argued the coat could have been accidentally contaminated either as a result of a policeman putting his hand in the pocket while searching or in the police photographic studio where the coat was taken prior to forensic testing for the taking of a photograph. Guns and ammunition had been stored in that studio. Contamination could even have occurred in the area of Keeley's laboratory. The methods of preventing contamination there were explored right down to the Henry Hoover vacuum cleaner used.

Keeley was unhappy that the coat had been taken to the studio. He agreed that there was a possibility that the coat had become contaminated in the photographic studio, but felt that it was most unlikely. He felt that innocent contamination was most unlikely to have occurred.

Fellow Forensic Science Service colleague Doctor Renshaw agreed with him.

The overall impression given was that the FDR came from the same gun which killed Jill. The only question seemed to be how it got to be in Barry's coat pocket.

That evidence would take up to three days as Mansfield grilled the police and scientists.

A single polyester fibre was also found on Jill's coat which could have come from Barry's trousers. This was claimed to show a two way link between Barry and Jill Dando.

Mark Webster, a forensic scientist for the Defence said that the finding of a single fibre was not reliable. It was too small for the dye to be analysed, and it was of a very common type.

On the day of the murder Barry visited the Hammersmith and Fulham Advice centre, or HAFAD. He also called to a taxi cab office where he managed to cadge a free trip to the Rickett Street Colon Cancer Clinic. Two days later he re-visited HAFAD and the taxi office, asking staff to recall what he had been wearing on the previous visit.

That strange behaviour was reported to the police. Barry at first told the police he did not know at what time he visited HAFAD but staff put the time at or before 12.00. Barry then claimed an alibi based on those times. If he had visited at or before 12.00 he would be ruled out as the killer, as the clothes he had on then did not match the clothes seen on the fleeing man in Gowan Avenue. He would not have had time to kill Jill at 11.30 and return home to change and still arrive at HAFAD for 12.00.

Under cross examination some of the staff revised their estimate of the time of Barry's visit but one, Susan Bicknell, was absolutely adamant that he had been there at 12.00.

To counteract the HAFAD alibi the police produced Julia Moorhouse who had reported being spoken to by a man matching Barry's description at about 12.30 on the day of the crime. Ms Moorhouse was not asked to attend an I.D. parade.

Other high profile trials were also then in progress at the Old Bailey. Sarah Ferguson's ex assistant Jane Andrews was found guilty of murdering her boyfriend and Lord Jeffrey Archer was back in court accused of perjury.

On June 8 Tony Blair and New Labour were re-elected, and in Ireland we rejected the Nice Treaty. (We would accept it when forced to vote again) I was waiting to return to London for the end of Barry's trial, and I stocked up on a few weeks supply of dog food for Shannon.

Meanwhile Hamish Campbell was giving evidence and he dismissed as unrealistic and simple a police intelligence report alleging Serbian involvement in the murder of Jill.

Defence

I was back at the Old Bailey on Wednesday 13 at 11.00 and I recorded it in my diary as a boring day. By now I would travel from Margaret's alone, ahead of Michelle as I liked to get in early before the cameramen were alert. I noticed that Michelle was by now quite blasé about them but I never liked their attention. I would ignore their occasional taunts when they would try for some reaction and I would try to look as impassive as possible. I would then have a cup of tea and a sandwich in the court cafeteria, and it also gave me a chance to cool down and read my newspaper.

The proceedings that day were rather tedious and revolved around whether Barry should give evidence. It has been described as a trial within a trial, a Section 35 they called it. Three doctors for the defence gave their opinions on Barry, Susan Young, Gisely Gudjohnson and Michael Kopelman. Doctor Elizabeth Logan gave evidence for the prosecution. Pownall was no match for the doctors and when he asked Gudjohnson if Barry was faking Gudjohnson simply asked 'faking what?' Logan was grilled by Mansfield. 'Is it customary for you to shout at your patients' he asked? He then went on to say that Logan could be heard through closed doors shouting at Barry in the court holding cells. Logan had written a report for the Crown claiming that Barry was very dangerous. The confidential report was later leaked to the press and was published in the Times after the trial ended.

We believed that if Barry gave evidence he would drift away in his attempt at explaining things, as he does. That is something that people who know him well understand, and find somewhat frustrating. But a jury might form the opinion that he was being deliberately evasive, dodging the question. Gage ruled that Barry could decide not to give evidence if he chose, and that no negative inference should be drawn from that. It was a great relief to us, and his defence team were delighted. I do not know if Barry shared our delight, I think he would have liked to have his say.

The jury were brought in after lunch and Mansfield began his opening address.

'The case against this Defendant is hanging by the merest of threads. The Prosecution have attempted over the previous weeks to erect an evidential edifice based upon a "speck" or particle no greater than 11.5 microns in size. Put another way, it is half of 1000th of an inch-invisible to the naked eye. Not only is it invisible but by the end of the case it will have disappeared altogether. Without it the Prosecution would have no case at all, for there is no other evidential link between this crime and this Defendant'.

The crime was he said committed in a professional manner by a professional hitman, planned and carefully executed. The window of opportunity was extremely narrow; she was shot within 30 seconds of leaving and alarming her car.

No witness identified Barry or anyone else hanging around near number 29 in the vital 30 minutes before her death, despite a number of witnesses being in Gowan Avenue during that time period. Nine witnesses including Mrs Upfill-Brown, a local doctor and Stella and Charlotte de Rosnay were out walking between 11 and 11.30. None of the nine saw anything untoward. He suggested that the killer was sitting in a vehicle along with an accomplice who when Jill arrived drove away to a rendezvous nearby.

The assailant had the element of surprise and came up on her from behind as she reached with her right hand to put the keys in her door lock which was to the left of the door. He grabbed her right forearm bruising it as he forced her down to doorstep level and holding the gun in his left hand shot her.

Mansfield then suggested that the Serbs might have shot her in retaliation for her Kosovo appeal and the NATO bombing of the headquarters of Radio Television Serbia in Belgrade. The station was owned and run by the Milosevic family and was seen as the main purveyor of Serbian State propaganda. (The station was in fact run but not owned by Milosevic's daughter) Jill Dando had become the public face of the BBC. Following the murder there were 5 or 6 phone calls to the BBC claiming a link between the Belgrade bombing and Jill's murder and making threats against her BBC boss Mr Tony Hall.

One of the calls which were never traced went as follows. 'Yesterday I called you to tell you to add a few numbers to the list. Because your Government and in particular your Prime Minister Blair, murdered, butchered, 17 innocent young people who work, like make-up artists, electrical and technical engineers and these type of people. He butchered, we butcher back. The first you had yesterday, the next one will be Tony Hall'. (Tony Hall went into hiding for some weeks after that threat)

In the autumn of 1999 the N.C.I.S. (National Criminal Intelligence Service) gave Hamish Campbell an intelligence report suggesting that Serbian Warlord Arkan ordered a hit on Jill and suggested the countries the assassin had travelled through and how he had arrived in the UK.

A member of the public pointed out to the police that ammunition made in Yugoslavia was routinely crimped.

Mansfield suggested that the assassin had discovered her Gowan Avenue address and assumed she would be leaving the house for work in the morning and so waited around in a vehicle. (Susan Mayes had seen a man standing by a burgundy double parked car who made her suspicious near Jill's house at 07.00. Another witness Kiela Hartigan had seen a blue Range Rover at 07.10 with a man in it parked nearby. A Traffic Warden Breege Clancy saw a parked blue Range Rover nearby with a man sitting in it)

Jill had also presented Crimewatch between 1995 and 1999. There was a high conviction rate in the cases which she personally presented. An aggrieved individual might have shot her in an attempt to curtail the programme.

He referred to the presumption of innocence when a Defendant pleads not guilty. It was up to the Crown to prove guilt to the jury's satisfaction, not for the defence to prove otherwise.

Firearms

The Remington bullet was crimped and Mansfield suggested that indicated that the killer came from an Eastern-Bloc country where crimping is commonplace. Barry had denied to police ever owning a gun or having access to them though he had been in the TA and had tried to join a gun club.

Turning to the FDR evidence he said that it was one of five types commonly encountered by experts and could have come from any point 38 ammunition containing the same primer constituents.

The Defence case was that the lone particle could no longer provide relevant or reliable evidence from which any inference could be drawn due to the mishandling of Barry's coat by police prior to forensic testing, which exposed the coat to the *real* risk of contamination.

No other particle was found, either at Barry's home or on his other clothing and so it appeared that the particle found in his coat was as a result of 'innocent contamination'. It was remarkable that no other particles were found at his home if he returned, as the Crown claimed, within minutes of the shooting with a highly contaminated weapon and or clothing in order to change and leave again. It must also have been the Crown's case that he did not come into possession of the gun for the first time on April 26 1999. It must be their case that he had possessed the gun and fired it before that date which would make it more likely that residue would be found in his home. But no gun or ammunition was found there; just a replica submachine gun which no one claimed was involved.

Identification

Mansfield then turned to witness identification of Barry and pointed out the dangers of misidentification and how it had plagued the justice system. The first Court of Criminal Appeal was set up in 1907 following the mistaken identification of Alfred Beck by 15 witnesses. A major inquiry into the risks of wrongful convictions as a result of misidentification was carried out by Lord Devlin in 1976.

No one identified Barry as the gunman. The only way the Crown could arrive at a purported identification would Mansfield claimed undermine all the protections and guidelines put in place over the years. The Crown was keen to show that the man seen by

Susan Mayes was the same man as spotted by the de Rosnay's, Terry Normanton, and the two eye-witnesses Mr Hughes and Mr Upfill-Brown. The problem with that was that the witnesses were highly divergent in their descriptions. Susan Mayes made a positive identification while Mr Hughes and Mr Upfill-Brown made no identification. Therefore the Crown seemed to be asserting that there was identification whether a witness identified, didn't identify, or wasn't sure. The Crown seemed to be saying that it was better to concentrate on the descriptions given which the Prosecution claimed had an underlying unity. That, Mansfield claimed not only made a nonsense of the procedures but was evidentially fallacious.

There were he said serious reservations made about four witnesses.

- The car seen by Susan Mayes was untraced and there was no evidence that Barry could drive or had access to a vehicle.

- It was only after a huge delay that Terry Normanton was able to communicate anything of what she had seen, and what she had seen appears to fit, in her words, 'the E-Fit exactly'. She said in cross examination that had the E-Fit been presented on the video parade she would have identified that person as the one she had seen. 'The problem for the Crown is that person is not the Defendant'.

- The Crown laid great emphasis on the underlying unity of descriptions of the man being of Mediterranean appearance. When asked if the man they saw had a Mediterranean appearance or olive skin the de Rosnay's both said that he did not.

- Neither Mr Hughes nor Mr Upfill-Brown described the man they saw as being of Mediterranean appearance.

Prosecution witnesses from HAFAD made written records of Barry's attendance on April 26 and 28. The times they recorded precluded him from being the killer, as he would not have had time to return home to change his clothes after the murder and be at HAFAD by noon.

Motive

While there was no obligation on them the Crown's case was singularly lacking a motive. There was no evidence that prior to Jill Dando's murder Barry had any particular interest in her.

He did not meet or attempt to meet her, try to contact her, follow or stalk her or hang around outside her house hoping to meet her.

He had no photographs of her, no fan type material, video footage, or the Radio Times for the week in which she died.

Out of 800 old newspapers only 8 predating her death had articles relating to her, and none of them had been marked or highlighted, circled, cut out, put to one side or filed.

Nobody who knew him recalled him going around speaking about or being obsessed with her, or claiming she had done him or Freddie Mercury some disservice.

Without any evidence of motive the prosecution could hardly say that given his willingness to engage in long tedious conversations that any obsession with Jill Dando had been kept secret.

Defence evidence

'We will endeavour to place evidence before you following the same chronology adopted by the Crown:-

- Eyewitnesses from the 26th April.

- The Defendant's movements.

- Experts concerned with fibres, firearms and residues.

None of this evidence will include the Defendant himself'.

The last line which meant that Barry would not be giving evidence was seen as a clever move as most of the reporters go away early on Friday's and so it did not receive any adverse publicity.

In the afternoon there was an amusing but important occurrence. While the junior defence barrister Maryam Syed was questioning window cleaner Alan Taylor Mr Mansfield passed a message to her via Marilyn Etienne. The window cleaner and the jury were then sent out while the question was aired. It simply was 'did the window cleaner have a ladder with him in Gowan Avenue on the morning of the murder?' He had been cleaning windows at the top floor of a house, and apparently he saw a man which another witness, Terry Belinda Normanton claimed to have seen. Terry recalled seeing a window cleaner up a ladder. The cleaner was called back and Maryam asked him 'did you have a ladder?' 'No' he replied curtly in a strong cockney accent, and the whole court burst into laughter. The jury was then called in, and the question was repeated. 'No' he repeated, and Maryam almost collapsed as laughter again broke out.

The reason for the question was not clear to me then, but Terry was certain she saw Barry on that same morning. If she believed that she saw the cleaner up a ladder which he did not have, could we trust her accuracy when she claimed to be so sure she had seen Barry? Incidentally the man they both saw was a gas meter reader.

Another man, Mr Williams described how he saw a man dash across Fulham Palace Road at about the time of the murder. To save himself from being run down he grabbed hold of a pole in the central island. Mr Williams reported it to the police and they fingerprinted the pole. He continued 'ten months later they took the bloody pole away, now we have one black one and one white one'. More laughter ensued.

Margaret was remaining positive and Barry phoned her on Saturday and again on Sunday. On the Sunday she asked him what he would like for his dinner when he came home and he said mash and fried onions, but could not think what meat he might like. I busied myself doing a few minor repairs around the house and met some other relatives in the Wishing Well.

On Monday Mansfield turned to the single particle of firearms discharge residue, FDR, which was apparently found in an inside pocket of Barry's Cecil Gee coat. That evidence has always been hotly contested, due to the mishandling of the coat prior to forensic testing.

Forensic Scientist Doctor John Lloyd was scathing of police procedures. He described the precautions that should be taken if searching for explosives, and said the same should apply where evidence of firearms residue would assume such importance. He said that some laboratories would not even report the finding of a single particle. He concluded that the single particle was not reliable due to 'flawed police procedures'.

(At the 1991 successful appeal of the Birmingham Six a report prepared by Doctor Lloyd completely undermined the forensic evidence which had secured the convictions, i.e. the positive Greiss tests carried out by Doctor Skuse)

In the evening Margaret exploded in fury at something and Michelle and I had to run for cover. The tension was now almost unbearable as the trial neared its end.

On Tuesday Major Freddy Mead gave his opinion on six crimp marks found on the cartridge case. He said it was common practice in what used to be known as Eastern Bloc countries to crimp bullets, so as to keep them secure while enduring vibration while being transported over rough roads or as may be caused by discharging fully automatic weapons. Pownall suggested that a one shot killing was not professional, and the Major replied 'it would be hard to imagine how it could have been bettered'.

It appeared that the forensic argument had been well and truly won by the defence. Maryam Syed explained to us that the single particle was one of the legs on which the case depended, and she appeared to think that Barry would be cleared as a result.

Not to be outdone Pownall appealed to Gage that this put the Crown at a disadvantage, and requested that the particle be downgraded in importance. Gage agreed to consider the request overnight. The defence ended, and the court finished early.

That evening Michelle and I met Margaret Renn, who advised us on how to deal with the media in the aftermath of the trial. We also began to plan a strategy for Barry's release. Later I said to Michelle that as Margaret Renn was so helpful we should consider giving her an interview.

Closing addresses

Crown

Pownall began his closing address to the jury on Wednesday, after Mr Justice Gage ruled that the case no longer depended on the single particle of FDR residue but that it could provide support for the identification. The goalposts seemed to have been changed in the middle of the match and I thought that was very unfair. The particle was the 'compelling evidence' and it had formed one of the three main planks on which the case rested. I.e. witness identification, the single particle, and at what time Barry visited HAFAD on the day of the murder. It would now merely assist the jury in reaching their decision. *Bad news*, I thought.

Pownall's style up to then was slow and ponderous, unlike the flamboyant Mansfield, but he was anything but boring in his summing up.

He absolutely rubbished the defence. He advised them that in the weeks to follow they might be conscious of both forensics and blue Range Rovers, which featured large in the case.

He was dismissive of the possibility that the firearms residue found in Barry's coat pocket got there as a result of innocent contamination. 'We submit that it is so unlikely that you can safely ignore the possibility of innocent contamination.' He would refer to names or events and then say 'don't speculate'. He was scathing of the possibility of Serb involvement. Why would they want to kill Jill?

Would Mr Arkan know her he asked mockingly, referring to the Kosovo war. Why not hit the BBC in Belgrade if that was what they wanted? The Kosovor's would like to blame the Serbs. No code word was used in the phone calls which claimed responsibility, and no award was claimed.

He turned dismissively to the police intelligence report and pointed to four lines which referred to a north London crime-family.

When Barry called back to HAFAD on April 28 1999 he said that friends had told him that he looked like the E-Fit of the suspect, but the E-Fit was not issued until April 30. Barry was seen in the area around the time of the crime wearing clothes which matched witness descriptions.

Barry had approached a reporter, Amanda Stocks, as she walked around Fulham some time after Jill's murder. Amanda found him to be chatty, approachable.

'The defendant chose not to give evidence, he remains unchallenged', he said. He mentioned the unidentified wet footprint which was found on Jill's doorstep, though it did not match Barry's shoes. He wondered why Barry did not have the copy of the Radio Times which showed the strange front and back cover which when opened out could have appeared to say: **Couldn't you just kill—Jill Dando**.

Pownall seemed to suggest that Barry must have had it. He drew everything tightly together from a broad web and made it sound convincing and damming. He certainly does his job well. (As Michelle and I went upstairs for a cup of tea she said to me 'my God, if I didn't know better he would almost have me convinced') Pownall made repeated references to the fact that Barry was in the dock but choose not to give evidence. I thought that was unfair as Mr Justice Gage had ruled that no negative inferences should be drawn from Barry's decision. Pownall ended.

Defence

'There is a chill wind blowing through this court, perhaps it has not reached the jury yet. We can turn the heat up'. So began Mansfield loudly, referring both to the air conditioning which was indeed a bit chilly, and the atmosphere as defined by Pownall. The large sword was back on the wall behind Gage, signifying that he was once again the senior judge sitting in court at the Old Bailey at that time.

'Anybody who is old enough will remember where they were during the Cuban missile crisis, when Princess Diana died, when Jill Dando was shot. I am not reading this out to you' he continued in contrast to Pownall's carefully scripted speech.

'If Barry was in HAFAD between 11.00 and 12.00, or may have been, you must acquit. If you are unsure of identification you must acquit'. He asked where Barry might have been hiding in the half hour prior to the murder and theatrically springing up he exclaimed 'was he in the dustbin, well, where *was* he?' A lot of people including the local doctor had given evidence that they had passed Jill's house during the half hour prior to her murder and saw nothing unusual.

He described the search of Barry's flat as a 'Higgledy Piggledy' operation. Some police had changed into their search clothes at home, some in the police van, some in the police station. They were not asked if they had been on a firearms course until much later, after the single particle was found.

'Why did they photograph the coat, it was never shown to witnesses. What did they find at his flat? I'll go quickly through it. They found no gun no ammunition no particles no traces no tools no workshop', he said at breakneck speed, causing the stenographer to smile as she struggled to keep up 'It would not be living in the real world if that was the first time that he had fired that gun. The evidence as a whole leads to a hole into which the particle disappears.'

He turned to the killing and remarked that no fibres had transferred from Barry's coat to Jill, though it was alleged that he forced her to the ground. If he was hanging around since 07.00 he would have wet shoes, but the footprint found did not match his.

'Why was the cartridge crimped', he asked, adding that it was the signature of the killer. 'In the USA the ATF, that's the alcohol tobacco and firearms agency, an unusual combination, and the Los Angeles Police Department agreed that the crimping was a trademark of the assassin. An assassin would not bring a weapon into the UK. The killing was an execution emanating from the war which was going on at the time'.

He recalled how fifty police officers kept Barry and his flat under surveillance with a camera trained on his front door. 'He didn't remove articles from his flat. He didn't attempt to hide or run away. The prosecution says he didn't have the copy of the Radio Times with Jill on the cover. But they mean Ah, but he had really. They can't have it both way's', he said loudly.

He drew to a close. 'The Crown case is trying to turn things into something their not. They are trying to turn him into something he's not'. He ended.

On Saturday Michelle and I visited Belmarsh. Barry was over the moon and nearly broke my hand with his handshake. He was extremely happy and spoke of his plans for his release. He expected that he would be compensated for his ordeal, and we did not contradict him. We had already been told that he probably would not get very much compensation as it could be argued that he was partly responsible for attracting the attention of the police in the first place. Unusually the staff at Belmarsh seemed to be friendly this time, and they even allowed us an extra half hour for our visit. We discussed plans that we had made for his first days of freedom. With the help of Margaret Renn a *safe* house was arranged with Camden Council, and the police would quickly rush him out the back entrance of the Old Bailey to try to escape the Media.

Judge's summing up

In this description I have quoted a section of the 2008 Appeal Court Approved Judgement, number 47.

On Monday June 25 Mr Justice Gage began his summing up. I was in court, but did not sit through all of it. The hourly breaks which were allowed for Barry were a relief to me. It was hot and oppressive in there and I would take any opportunity to get a break. I was constantly aware of the presence of the Dando camp and police behind me, though I guess they were not in the least interested or aware of me.

The courtroom is served by a twin set of double doors with a small area between them. I was standing in there observing the court when a girl from the Securior prison service was shown in to have a look. When Barry was pointed out to her she was aghast and exclaimed 'Oh that's Barry George, Oh God, interesting, very interesting'. I tried to keep a straight face as she left, looking as if she had seen a monster. The media campaign to demonise Barry had obviously been very effective.

I thought Gage gave a fair summing up. He was a senior 'Red Robe' judge, and for a time I suspected that he was carefully selected to ensure there could be no challenge to the fairness of the trial. To the best of my knowledge his last two cases had failed to deliver verdicts.

He described the expert evidence in relation to the FDR as being important to the Prosecution case against Barry.

The evidence of Robin Keeley and Doctor John Lloyd was very important he said.

The finding of the FDR provided support for the other evidence that Barry was the murderer.

He described the identification issue, the attempt to create a false alibi and the FDR as the three main strands of the case

He said: ' . . . you might be left in a position where you are sure that the prosecution has proved the identification part of its case and disproved the alibi and proved the added factor that he tried to fabricate an alibi, but you are not sure that the particle of fire arm residue has been proved to be other than innocent, and I hope you understand when I use the shorthand expression 'innocent'. In that event the prosecution still contend that you can draw the necessary inference that the defendant was the killer. The defence say the particle of fire arms discharge residue is so important to the prosecutions case that you could not possibly find him guilty if that strand of the prosecutions case is not proved.

In those circumstances, you would have to be very careful and cautious before concluding that the prosecution has proved that he was the murderer.'

Appeal Court Approved Judgement.2008.

He asked if they were sure the particle was not left on the coat as a result of innocent or adventitious contamination. Mr Keeley's and Doctor John Lloyds evidence was of very considerable importance. He directed the jury that they should consider the FDR evidence on its own and only have regard to it if they were sure that it did not come from innocent contamination. If they were sure that it did not come from innocent contamination then they could consider it along with all the other evidence. If they were not sure then an important part of the case was removed.

He said to ignore the use of the term 'The Defendant' by Susan Mayes. He questioned her accuracy. On Terry Belinda Normanton he said there were discrepancies, and to consider her evidence very carefully. He pointed to Barry's approach to the postman six weeks after the murder saying I've just seen the killer.

He went over witness's descriptions and asked if there was a continuity of descriptions, an underlying unity or disunity. As regards HAFAD he said 'Lies do not prove guilt'. He pointed out that Barry had 29 days military training with the TA and had 'Probably' fired rifles.

Barry had shown a positive dislike for the BBC. The 'Special Lady' Barry had evidently referred to could have been Jill Dando. He had said to the reporter Amanda Stocks that Jill was a 'Lovely Lady'.

Gage then referred to a conversation that Barry had in a Fulham hairdressers. While Barry was talking about how he feared the police suspected him a hairdresser asked him 'did you kill her?' Barry looked down at the floor and appeared to be muttering quietly, but didn't answer the question. That could support the Crowns case, Gage said.

The summing up ended on Wednesday. The key question Gage said was 'is Susan Mayes accurate?' She had made the only positive unqualified ID. He said he required a unanimous verdict, and told the jury to elect a foreman. They should only discuss the case in the jury room. He warned them to be careful with the exhibit guns smiling as he said 'they are not loaded, but they could still hurt'. I do not know if there really were guns there or not. The jury would be accommodated in a local hotel until they were finished deliberating. They went out at 10.40.

I thought things were looking good, but a depressing meeting with the defence team on the previous Tuesday nagged at me. If the jury failed to reach a verdict Pownall would go for a re-trial in August. Mansfield stated bluntly 'the prosecution always come back stronger'. If Barry was convicted we should make no comment pending an appeal. Even if he was cleared we should say little due to proposed changes in the 'Double Jeopardy' rule. This would mean that a defendant could be tried again if acquitted, providing new evidence emerged.

I expected the jury to come back quickly. On Thursday I warned Margaret to be prepared for a verdict. It was 'Kosovo Day' and it was reported that the Serbian President Slobodan Milosevic had been arrested and was on his way to The Hague. At 15.30 the call came over the public address: 'All parties in George to court number one'. The cafeteria emptied as everybody made their way down to the courtroom. The adrenalin was pumping as we filed into court. Maryam Syed whispered to us that it was not a verdict, the jury just wanted to ask a question. Relax again and drink more tea.

The street outside the Old Bailey was thronged with reporters that evening and I found that I could not bear to run the gauntlet. I was not feeling the best, so Michelle and I waited an hour until they were gone and then made our way to a pub on the corner which serves a nice pint of Guinness, and even has a resident ghost, though I never did meet it. But the Guinness did revive my spirits.

Friday marked the eight week of the trial. It was decided that the court would sit on Saturday. On Friday evening I mentioned to Margaret the possibility of a re-trial. 'I thought he was getting off' she snapped. 'Something has gone wrong, their taking too long', I replied.

On Saturday the station at Saint Paul's was closed, and a bus took us from Holborn to Liverpool Street station. Unfortunately the bus driver did not know the stops for the stations in between. A BBC woman who may have been from Crimewatch allowed us to share her taxi back to the court. We got out before the taxi reached the court entrance, and the BBC woman followed some distance behind us as we walked to the door. We were mobbed by the cameramen again. The woman was shocked, and said to me as we went through the security checks 'Good God, it's a liability following you lot, all those cameras'.

As we sat in the cafeteria whiling the morning away a woman approached and introduced herself as Ann Moneypenny from MOJO. I thought she looked like Ann Robinson of the Weakest Link. She was dressed all in black with a glass crucifix hanging from her neck. I was surprised as MOJO had never responded to the letter which

I had written to them back in April. We chatted away as we whiled away the morning waiting for a call to go back to Court Number One. She told us that she was an agent for pop stars, actresses etc before she joined MOJO.

That Saturday was a dreary one as Barry's case seemed to be the only case on that day. Hamish Campbell was sat near to us, and the Dando camp was as far away from us as space would allow. I thought some of the young ones seemed to be eyeballing me as I brought tea to our table, but I ignored it. We never spoke with the Dando camp, as the media were always watching our every move. Though we did not consider it a case of them and us the fact is that we were on opposite sides. I would like to think that we all just wanted justice, but life is never that simple. That court case was not about truth and justice in my opinion, but about whether or not a conviction could be secured. One day during a tea break I was on the brink of making an approach to Alan Farthing, but I could not think of what to say, so I said nothing. When I looked back from my spot in the courtroom our eyes met but we did not speak.

When lunchtime came the Dando camp left the building but we remained. We did not want to give the cameramen any opportunity. After lunch Mansfield and the rest of the defence team met Michelle and I in the solicitor's room which is adjacent to the cafeteria. Mansfield asked Doctor Susan Young to demonstrate her relaxation techniques. We all had our eyes closed concentrating on our breathing when somebody groaned. Maryam Syed exploded in laughter and we all fell about the place. We tried again and we drifted away to somewhere nice in our memories, far away from the hothouse which is the Old Bailey. I found myself with Shannon in the fields close to the ruins of an old Norman castle near where I live. Suddenly the door opened and the Ann Robinson look-alike Moneypenny stuck her head in. The room again exploded into laughter. Mansfield was then called to reception where his wife Yvette was waiting. She brought us tea and biscuits and we relaxed and settled down for a nice chat. 'All parties in George to court number one'. Michelle and I jumped, startled; we were back to reality with a bang. We all filed down again expecting the verdict, but it was just Mr Justice Gage giving the jury directions for Sunday, when they would have a day off. They could either stay in their hotel or go on a coach trip to the countryside.

Sunday was to be one of the most miserable days I have ever experienced in London. In the afternoon I walked to the Du Cane Road bus shelter where somebody had written graffiti in support of Barry. Later we watched a video, the excellent My Fair Lady. We forgot our troubles for a little while as Eliza Doolittle's father lamented the imminent loss of his freedom as he sang 'I'm Getting Married in the Morning.' Margaret remained very uptight waiting for the verdict. She never came to court and we did not encourage her due to the media interest.

Monday July 3. At about 11.00 I met Paddy Hill in a pub opposite the Old Bailey. We had tea and coffee and a good chat. He spoke of his many years in prison doing time for a crime that he did not commit, and of the excitement of his release.

At 12.50 I went back to the court and asked Michelle to come out for lunch. Michelle, Moneypenny, Paddy and I then walked down the street four abreast to the delight of the cameramen. We were silently giving out the message that if Barry was convicted we would not be going away quietly. We had lunch of chicken and chips in the Café Rouge and then we returned to the court. Paddy Hill would not come inside.

At 15.50 Maryam Syed told us that the jury had again asked to see Barry's coat in which the single particle of firearms residue was found. We were relaxed, lounging around in the cafeteria just waiting now for the jury to fail to agree a verdict. Moneypenny popped out to deposit my camera film with a developer as it contained interesting shots of the Du Cane Road graffiti. 'All parties in George to court number one'. I was slightly surprised as it was just past 16.00 and the court would usually sit until 16.30. Another question perhaps? It seemed too early to be going home. We casually made our way down again but when we reached the outer doors it was apparent that something was different. The place was mobbed, and I heard a reporter say on her mobile phone 'it's a verdict'. I looked up at the public gallery and it was full. The atmosphere seemed thick and heavy as we took our seats.

Michelle sat between Moneypenny and me. 'All rise' said the court clerk and Mister Justice Gage came in, bowed and sat. Barry came up from the holding cells. Then the jury filed in, all eleven of them. One had had to leave due to bereavement. I looked at the jury hoping to see a smile but was dismayed to see that they looked

97

furious, angry or upset. I once read that a jury which is going to acquit may look happy, but these did not look happy. Anything but. The tension was unbearable as we waited for the young black foreman to give the verdict. 'Guilty'. There was a loud gasp from behind us which I assume was from the Dando camp. It was certainly not from Michelle, as has been reported. Barry was sentenced to life in prison, and was quickly taken down. We barely saw him as they moved him so fast.

Michelle phoned a message for somebody to break the news to her mother, but she was already watching it on a news flash. 'Give that lot nothing', Moneypenny said referring to the media. We were last to leave the courtroom and the cleaner was sweeping up. He told Michelle off for using her mobile phone. We went and had a cup of tea. Dr Susan Young came to us and advised Michelle to let solicitor Marilyn Etienne read the prepared statement. It was feared Michelle might break down while reading it. We fought our way through the dense crowd outside the Old Bailey to the microphones where Etienne announced 'No One Has Received Justice' and revealed that Barry would be seeking leave to appeal. We re-entered the Old Bailey and Paddy Hill accompanied us. 'That's the door we went out, that one there' he shouted to the bemused police, referring to the release of the Birmingham Six.

We met with Mansfield, and he looked really shocked as he explained the appeal process to us. He advised us not to talk to the press and to just say to reporters 'No Comment Pending Appeal'. I later read that he walked seven miles all the way to his home in a bid to try and make sense of it all. We said our goodbyes and made our way to the back of the building where an unmarked police car was waiting. They drove Michelle, Moneypenny and I back to East Acton. Michelle was slightly miffed with me for offering mints to the police, which they accepted. The photographers were at Margaret's gate but the police and Moneypenny got rid of them. Moneypenny stayed for a few hours and helped persuade Margaret to go to Ireland for a while to get away from it all. It was a difficult evening, and we could not even watch the news in case it upset Margaret further.

Cause celebre

2001-'02

The following morning I ran a gauntlet of reporters as I fed the parking meter outside Margaret's house. I walked to the shops to get milk and the papers. I handed some MOJO business cards to waiting reporters and fielded questions by repeating 'no comment pending appeal' and explained that we would not be able to visit Barry as we did not have a visiting order.

I sat outside the back of Margaret's house in the sunshine reading the papers. The Telegraph's editorial read 'If ever a case needed the imprimatur of a higher court this is one' while the Daily Mail's read 'It would be a bitter blow if this became another of those high profile cases which come back to haunt the reputation of British Justice.'

About lunchtime there was a knock on the door. We were expecting Moneypenny to call and so thinking somebody I knew was outside

I opened it and to my surprise found a TV camera in my face. The camera was obviously recording as the female reporter thrust a microphone at me. If I retreated it would have looked as if we were hiding away, skulking behind closed doors, so I stepped out keeping my left hand inside the door to prevent getting locked out. The reporter asked me something and ignoring the question I said 'he shouldn't have gone down, he's innocent'. That I felt, was the truth. Margaret Renn had advised me to say Innocent rather than Not Guilty to avoid any possible tampering with a recording. I then lowered my voice so that the microphone could not pick up my voice, speaking politely with the reporter. Suddenly my hand was grabbed and Michelle dragged me back into the house. She was absolutely furious with me and said that I should not have spoken and should have slammed the door in their faces. I don't think that would have looked very good on the news. Margaret was also angry with me and said 'this is my house, I decide what happens here. Its over, I want to hear no more about it'. I was definitely now in the dog house, trapped with two angry women.

On the lunchtime news my surprise at being faced by the camera was apparent but at least I wasn't shown being dragged back inside. The message was out; we were not accepting the jury's verdict. Another relative then phoned me and gave out stink because I was seen on TV. 'I am not going to hide behind closed doors; I think he is innocent and we are going to fight this' I retorted. I seemed to be getting on the wrong side of everybody now. Later Moneypenny called around and got rid of the couple of reporters who were still hanging around. We were puzzled over a public statement made by MOJO's John McManus which appeared to pour cold water on Barry's appeal prospects. He said it would be difficult to find grounds for appeal as Barry was convicted on mostly circumstantial evidence. It was not a positive statement. Moneypenny then made arrangements for somebody to pick up Sheba the cat which would be looked after while Margaret was in Ireland. Moneypenny was brilliant then, reassuring Margaret and Michelle and dealing with the media. I went over to the Wishing Well with her where we met reporter Amanda Stocks. I recognised Amanda as Michelle had pointed her out to me in the Old Bailey as she had thought that Amanda appeared to look a little hostile. But Amanda now seemed quite friendly and down to earth, quite a likeable person really. She felt a little ill due to the very warm day. I was puzzled, as she had been a prosecution witness and News of the World reporter. I asked Moneypenny if she was part of MOJO and she assured me that Amanda was ok. Later back at the house Moneypenny asked us did we have any nice photos of Barry as we needed to counteract the bad image portrayed by the press. I had some good ones which she liked.

It was agreed that Michelle and Margaret would travel with me in my car next day to Ireland where Michelle would be met in Cahir, County Tipperary. They would then go down to Cork and I would continue on my way home.

It was quite a stressful evening after Moneypenny left. As I would be leaving for Fishguard shortly after 07.00 I asked Margaret to pack her bag. 'I will do it in the morning' she said.

At about 21.30 I went to the Wishing Well for a few pints. When I got back to the house shortly after 23.00 everything seemed to have changed. Michelle popped down from upstairs and to my surprise told me that they would not be travelling to Ireland with me after all, as she had a TV engagement. They would fly over afterwards.

The following day she gave an interview to Martin Bashir for ITV's 'Tonight with Trevor McDonald' programme, while I drove home. At Leigh Delamere Service Station on the M4 I bought the Daily Mail. There was an article by Bob Woffinden which cast doubts on Barry's conviction, while Lynda Lee Potter wrote 'I have grave doubts as to the safety of Barry George's conviction'. Barry's situation was said to be becoming a 'cause celebre'. He would love that description, I thought. When I got home I got a huge frantic reception from Shannon.

I felt shattered after all that had happened but the next morning Shannon and I took a long walk through the hills and fields and I felt better. I looked forward to a nice relaxing pint in a local village, dinner and a little normality again.

Around lunchtime Michelle phoned and asked me would I bring my photos of Barry to Clonakilty, County Cork as MOJO were doing a photo shoot. I was a little surprised that she invited me along but I immediately said yes and drove the 90 miles there, looking forward to meeting the MOJO people again. I took the old winding road noticing the road signs along the way reminiscent of the civil war years, such as Crossbarry and Beal na mBlath where Michael Collins was ambushed and shot.

When I arrived at Clonakilty's plush Inchydoney Island Hotel I was met in the car park by Paddy Hill along with another man who I assumed incorrectly was part of MOJO. He asked me if I had brought the photos, and to my surprise he just glanced at them and put them in the boot of his car. I later discovered that he was a freelance photographer. Michelle and Margaret were upstairs in the hotel having tea and sandwiches with Moneypenny and again to my surprise Amanda Stocks. Margaret still seemed shell-shocked and Michelle was far too busy to talk to me. I noticed a micro tape recorder on the big table and I was hit by a feeling of dismay. I just knew this wouldn't end well. I tried to get my photos back but was fobbed off for the remainder of the day.

The Irish Independent ran a feature on the case on Saturday. Though the reporter gave an incorrect description of my house, saying it had hardly changed since the early 1950s when Margaret left for London he mitigated it by describing Shannon as a magnificent red setter. I was pleased to see her getting a good mention in a national paper.

On Sunday four of my photographs of Barry featured in the centrespread of the News of the World under the headline 'Imp Who Grew into a Devil'. I am not sure that Barry's public image was much improved by that.

In the Mail on Sunday and the News of the World Nick Ross wrote of his views on the verdict and of how he always knew that it was Barry or somebody very like him who killed Jill.

Meanwhile the Sunday Mirror carried the story of Barry's 1982 victim, how she was attacked after saying goodnight to her boyfriend who she later married. It made chilling reading, but though it was a terrible story it did not convince me that he had attacked Jill Dando seventeen years later.

'You must be psychic' Margaret Renn exclaimed on Wednesday when I phoned her, she had just been reaching for the phone to call me.

She advised me not to be too angry over the Clonakilty events and then she told me of her surprise when she walked into the BBC newsroom and how her amused colleagues pointed to the news screen which told of the Trevor McDonald/Martin Bashir programme. She had been told that she could not have an interview with us due to Mansfield's good advice.

Margaret Renn was very helpful to us before and during the trial and I feel she was treated shoddily in the end. She would continue to be a source of good advice to me in the years that followed, when Barry's case seemed to be forgotten.

On Saturday I spoke to Paddy Hill and he exploded in one of his customary outbursts. (As depicted in a Guardian article by Simon Hattenstone, June 17 2002)

I got the impression that I was not the most popular in his book but the feeling was mutual after the Clonakilty caper. On July 31

Michelle was interviewed by the late great Gerry Ryan on his RTE radio programme. Michelle described Barry as 'a regular fun guy'. Gerry then referred to putting a hand up a woman's skirt. I was not very impressed but I had no influence on RTE. I had sent them a request not to run the interview in keeping with Mansfield's advice, to no avail.

After the Clonakilty affair the unity amongst Barry's family supporters was fragmented and Michelle and I followed our independent paths for the rest of his incarceration and beyond. Michelle stayed within the MOJO camp which she found to be a source of help and support, and me outside but still in touch.

After Barry's conviction we were not in a position to visit him for some time and he did not contact us. I would write to him but he never replied. I had used up most of my holidays and quite a bit of special unpaid leave. Michelle had spent the whole of the trial away from her family while she attended court, and Margaret was not in a position to make the trip alone.

I do not know at first-hand how he dealt with his conviction. In his PRISON DIARY Jeffrey Archer records on Friday 20 July seeing a prisoner on exercise that looked totally lost. A fellow prisoner Gordon told Archer that it was Barry George. 'No one in here believes he did it, including the screws' Gordon said. Archer revealed that while his own trial was in progress he was surprised that so many senior lawyers and laymen told him that they were disturbed by the verdict.

Later a prison officer revealed to Archer that he didn't believe that Barry had shot Jill Dando. 'He's just too stupid' the officer said. A prisoner called Pat told Archer how a year earlier Barry had fallen over while running in the prison sports day. Pat described Barry as a bit of a pervert but believed that he was not a murderer.

Belmarsh is a holding prison for prisoners awaiting trial so shortly after his conviction Barry was moved to HMP Whitemoor, in Cambridgeshire. We were relieved that he was not moved too far away from London. During August it was reported that David Dobbins, a friend of Barry's who became a prosecution witness had hanged himself, preceded by his brother. I was told that David was depressed but I do not know if his giving evidence against Barry contributed to his unfortunate death. Finally on September 2 a visiting order arrived.

One day Tom and I were doing a little autumn tidying up outside our house. Tom went in for a cigarette, and when he came out he said that two planes had crashed into a building in New York City. I dismissed that as unlikely, thinking that maybe a single light aircraft had crashed. Then I went in for a cup of tea and I saw on Sky News the horror unfolding. It was September 11 or 9-11 as it became known. Two more planes would be crashed and up to 20,000 were feared dead. The official death toll was fixed at 2751 but many more would die as a result in the years which followed.

I later watched with disgust as the Twin Towers collapsed in a cloud of dust and rubble. It was awful to realise that people were dying there as we watched.

I was alarmed on Sunday 16 to read an article in the Mail on Sunday about an alleged hanging attempt by Barry. It was claimed that another prisoner Daniel Reese saved him.

On Wednesday September 26 Margaret and I made our first trip to HMP Whitemoor. We left East Acton at 10.00 and made our way to Kings Cross station where we took the train to Peterborough. Then we took the Stanstead Airport train across the bleak flat Fenlands to March station. From there we took a taxi to the prison, arriving at 13.00. The prison is built on the site of the former Whitemoor railway marshalling yards which were the largest in Europe. In 1994 six IRA prisoners armed with smuggled guns escaped but were later recaptured.

We found the staff at Whitemoor to be quite friendly, a refreshing change from the grim Belmarsh. The visiting area is spacious, with cameras hanging from the high ceiling. There are bolted down round tables and chairs, blue chairs for visitors and red for inmates. The Women's Royal Voluntary Service provides a snack bar where pre-paid vouchers can be exchanged for tea and snacks.

Barry came in after a little while. I was pleased to see that the awful beard was gone. He seemed well, and he reassured us that the recent press report about a hanging attempt were groundless. He appeared to be positive and he was looking forward to his appeal. He wondered if Gareth Peirce would represent him and I agreed to ask her. I got the teas in, and Barry had Coke, a Mars bar and prawn cocktail crisps.

The visit ended and we left Barry sitting at the table. I used to hate that part of the visits as I always felt that he shouldn't be there. We took the taxi back to March station.

On the way to Peterborough we sat with a volunteer prison visitor, a little old lady who was now worried about travelling due to terrorism. Everything had changed since 9-11, and the papers were full of scare stories about anthrax and chemical attacks. Gas masks were on sale for £60. I used to feel a little uneasy while travelling on the London underground in case of terrorist attacks in such a confined space. An old Chinese curse came to mind, 'May you live in interesting times'.

The next day I phoned Gareth Peirce who confirmed she would represent Barry if he so desired. (It would be over a year before he would make the change) Later I nearly had a panic attack when a MOJO member called to Margaret's. She said that what she was about to tell us could get her shot. It was an old horse-chestnut theory about a 1996 Chelsea F.C. helicopter crash. I sat there in Margaret's living room wondering might the door suddenly burst open, might we all get shot.

In October Moneypenny asked me to come to Cork to discuss a documentary with Channel 4. I drove down and to my surprise when I entered the hotel room a man who was introduced as James Cohen asked me if we would kick off the interview as the cameras were ready to roll. 'Come on now Michael, don't be shy', Moneypenny said when I was reluctant to be interviewed on camera. 'You tricked me once' I retorted angrily, 'you won't do it a second time'. James was shocked at the outburst and said he had thought I was agreeable. Instead of a recorded interview we agreed that I would assist them with background research for the planned Cutting Edge documentary.

On Sunday November 4 I was contacted by Andy Parr, an independent justice campaigner. He once campaigned for the Guildford Four, who spent many years in prison for a bombing they did not do, despite the real bombers admitting to the police that it was they who did it. Andy suggested that Margaret and I go to a public meeting which was planned for the House of Commons in November. He advised that we should never give up the struggle even though we would have setbacks.

Unknown to us on November 19 a meeting took place between the prosecution forensic expert witness Robin Keeley and the Forensic Science Service's Doctor Ian Evett. It was to have far reaching consequences but it would be another six years before its significance became apparent.

I went to London on November 25 as I was on a week's holiday. I immediately noticed that Margaret seemed to find my presence irritating, and I could seem to do nothing right in that week. On Monday Paddy Hill and Moneypenny visited us along with the TV team who were making the Cutting Edge documentary. James Cohen was the Director along with David Perrin. It was agreed that we would go to Whitemoor in a people carrier provided by Cutting

Edge, and they would film and interview Margaret along the way while I would remain off camera.

On Wednesday Margaret and I went on our first visit to the House of Commons. MOJO were there along with Andy Parr and families of prisoners who had died in police custody. We spoke to a few reporters but we did not think it achieved anything worthwhile. Moneypenny and Amanda Stocks were having a drink in a local pub when Fiona Cummins of the Daily Mirror spoke with me. I spoke to Fiona about the events which had occurred at Inchydoney Island the previous July. It was not reported but I was interested to see what looked to me like panic on the faces of Amanda and Moneypenny.

The next day we set off for Whitemoor along with James Cohen and the Cutting Edge team. As the young female production manager sped along hugging the fast lane of the motorway Sophie filmed Margaret while James spoke to her. 'Margaret what did you do this morning' he asked? 'I fed the cat, and Michael' she meekly whispered. I felt like going 'Woof Woof'.

During the visit Barry caused me some alarm by suggesting that he wanted to sack Mansfield, and I strongly advised him not to. I agreed to pass on a message from him to Gareth Peirce.

When we got back to Margaret's I found a press report dropped in by Margaret Renn about a previous case which involved a man called Ira Thomas who was convicted of a shooting. But the forensic evidence was later proved unreliable and Mr Thomas was released. That case helped ensure that Barry would get to have an appeal.

Overall it was a rather unpleasant week for me, and as I returned home on Friday 30 I heard the sad news on my car radio that George Harrison of The Beatles had died.

On Sunday December 9 the News of the World reported that Barry 'ogled' two female prison officers, and that he had requested an Ouija Board for to contact Jill Dando. I felt the report originated from within HMP Whitemoor and was designed to undermine his appeal application and so I wrote a strong letter of complaint to the prison Governor and the Home Secretary.

On Friday I heard on the radio that his appeal had been granted.

Michelle and Margaret visited him before Christmas and the Cutting Edge team went with them, but this time they took the train.

In early January 2002 a girl was shot in the head in a casual mobile phone robbery in East London, but fortunately she survived. Also in January the Daily Mail carried reports of sightings of a disgraced Gynaecologist called Rodney Ledward. They published comments made by some of his ex patients and a solicitor. But it later transpired Mr Ledward had died on October 19 2000. So much for the reliability of witness identifications I thought.

One evening I was reviewing some old news video, and I observed grainy footage of a man who was portrayed as Barry sitting in the park during the public vigil for Princess Diana. What drew my attention was that the man wore a watch along with a bracelet and gold rings. Barry claimed that he did not have a watch at the time of Jill Dando's murder, which happened two years later. When I later showed the video to Margaret and Michelle they were adamant that it was not Barry. David Perrin of Cutting Edge also showed it to Barry's friend Robert Charig, and he did not believe the man was Barry either.

In late January David Perrin came to visit me and we met in the local pub where we discussed Barry. I again said that I would not go on screen, but would otherwise co-operate. David came to see my house where as he said it all began. Shannon gave him her usual big welcome, but no muddy paw.

I was again in London on February 18 when DC Bartlett was cleared of harassing the witness Charlotte de Rosnay. Charlotte was reported to have had an affair with a policeman before the trial. Questions were also raised about her contact with the key witness Susan Mayes.

On Tuesday I met Margaret Renn for the last time at Bush House on the Aldwych. This was near where the Bulgarian dissident Georgi Markov was assassinated in the late seventies after leaving the BBC's Bush House. I remember that crime as I worked then on the number 11 bus which would often terminate at The Aldwych. Mr Markov was stabbed in the leg possibly by a Bulgarian KGB agent using an adapted umbrella tip which contained a slow acting poison, Ricin.

Margaret Renn took me to the Royal Courts of Justice, where Barry's appeal would be heard. It did not seem as intimidating as the Old Bailey. She asked me the question if Barry didn't do it then who did? I was stumped, having never given much consideration to that. But I would later.

On Wednesday my sister Margaret and I visited Barry. I had to stand all the way to Peterborough, and when we got to March Margaret suggested that we walk to the prison and back as the taxi cost £5. I was suffering from an injury to my foot, and the wind was howling over the Fenlands. We took the taxi.

There was an amusing incident when we entered the prison visiting hall. Margaret said 'look at the state of him', as she walked to a table. I glanced over and thought that Barry was much heavier looking than last time. A prison officer then called to her saying 'he's over there', and realising her mistake she turned away from the puzzled looking wrong man and went to the correct table where the real Barry sat. We were laughing as we sat down, but he was not.

He complained about a lack of support from us, and about his Legal team. I asked him if he had ever fired a gun in the TA and he said he hadn't. He asked me to check out the internet for information, and he got annoyed when I said I did not know how to do that. 'Any fool with a brain, with half a brain could use the internet', he said. He was very uptight and said that if we didn't help him and his appeal failed 'I will rot in here'.

I again met David Perrin on Thursday and we discussed the Cutting Edge programme.

As I returned home on Friday I heard that John Thaw had died. I liked him in the TV series Home to Roost.

I bought a new book by John McVicar and I thought it was hilarious as he explained 'How and why Barry George executed Jill Dando.' I had seen McVicar at the Old Bailey and noticed that he spoke to Michelle one day in the cafeteria. He recounted a brief conversation which he had with her. I thought the book was a bit silly but also quite informative. He gave a good description of the police and court proceedings, but it was made hilarious by Benji the binman and the Queen Music and Freddie Mercury theories. I felt sorry that his poor dog Clem had drowned in the Thames.

We next visited Barry on Easter Saturday and the security checks appeared to be more thorough than normal. Barry was very uptight again and refused to speak to us until the prison officers allowed us to move to another table. He feared that the first table was bugged. I noticed that he was not wearing shoelaces. He said that there was a prisoner who was willing to give evidence against him. I thought that he was becoming paranoid. During the period of our visit the Queen Mother died. When my mother would be feeling sorry for herself I would try to humour her by saying 'the Queen Mother is ten years older than you and she's still flying it.'

Confessions

2002

On Easter Sunday March 31 I took a walk around Fulham to see the scene of the crime. I felt a little uneasy walking past Jill's Gowan Avenue house and I didn't hang around. I walked from Munster Road to Fulham Palace Road near where my car was parked and then drove down Doneraile Street to Bishops Park. I was struck by how long this would take a fleeing killer on foot, and how long he would be exposed if this were his escape route. I walked around Bishops Park. The public toilet was open which was fortunate as I had drunk too much tea again. Could Barry have changed his clothes here and hidden the gun along the lines of McVicar's claim? Unlikely I thought, somebody would surely have found evidence of it. Looking across the river I observed all the small boats on the other side. After the murder a man was seen jumping over the parapet and I wondered if this could have been the escape route via a waiting small boat.

But that might be too much like James Bond. Apart from the toilet all the buildings that I saw in the park area appeared to be securely padlocked. So where was the building McVicar said Barry had access to? Where he said he changed his clothes before going on to HAFAD, after burying his gun in a previously prepared hole? It did not add up. I then drove past HAFAD and the Traffic Cars office.

Later in the week I mentioned to David Perrin how McVicar had wrote that Barry had deliberately got himself charged so as to later claim compensation. To my surprise he said that some people in Fulham who knew Barry also thought that.

On Sunday April 7 I heard on BBC Radio 4 news that the News of the World had a cassette tape of Barry apparently confessing to the murder. I bought the paper and read the story which I found difficult to believe. It alleged that Barry said to other prisoners ' . . . because I was the man who committed the murder'. I phoned the number given and listened to the tape recording which sounded like Barry though the sound quality was very poor. I had warned him that something like that could happen. The source of the tape was a by then deported Polish thief who claimed he used his tape recorder to record fellow prisoner's music.

In Monday's Daily Mirror Nigel Dando summed it up saying 'it would be a very interesting development if true'. But the damage was done. On Monday evening down at my local pub an old man could not contain himself. 'I saw it, he admitted it, I saw it in the News of the World', he said gleefully.

On the following Sunday I saw a report on BBCs Ceefax from Scotland Yard saying that reports that Barry was being investigated for the murder of the model Rachel Nickell on Wimbledon Common in 1992 were untrue. It referred to a Mail on Sunday report by Amanda Perthen which said that the 'downmarket' Sunday papers report on Barry's 'confession' was untrue, but that Daniel Reece, police informer and fellow prisoner had tapes of Barry describing how he had killed Jill Dando, and linking him to the Nickell murder. Reece had featured in the Mail on Sunday report shortly after Barry's conviction claiming to have saved Barry from hanging. Amanda had been in my house back in year 2000 when she worked for the Sunday People. I didn't rise to the bait then when she seemed to try to get me to say something negative about the police. In an unrelated comment the MP Keith Viaz once said 'you have to take everything the Mail on Sunday says with a pinch of salt'. I later complained to the Home Office about the prisoner's use of recording equipment.

On Saint George's day Margaret Michelle and I again went to the House of Commons to a public meeting. We met Moneypenny and Paddy Hill at Saint Stephens gate at 13.30. David Perrin was also there. James Cohen drifted loftily by lost in thought, his dark glasses perched high on his bald head.

John McDonnell MP met us inside. We discussed the abuse of press freedom and the appeal court's attitude to the CCRC. Paddy Hill said that things were now worse than when he was released back in 1991. He spoke of Susan May whose appeal had recently been dismissed. Susan was serving life after being convicted of murdering her Aunt. She enjoyed the support of 100 MPs. I am not sure what those meetings actually achieve though it is important that public support is demonstrated in disputed cases.

After the meeting we had a drink in Finnegan's pub off Victoria Street. They do coffee, and fill a good pint of Guinness. Later, at Saint James underground station one of the Cutting Edge people bizarrely handed me a dismantled 9mm bullet. I was surprised by the weight of the head. David Perrin asked me if I would reconsider giving Cutting Edge an interview and Margaret quickly answered for me saying 'NO he won't'. I would later worry a little over handling that bullet but there were no negative consequences.

On my way to the ferry at Holyhead I read in the Metro paper that a BBC female vet had been stalked and how she feared she would be a stalking victim like Jill Dando. A stalking victim? Perhaps, but I was not convinced that Jill was killed by a stalker.

During May Barry had a hernia operation. I upset David Perrin because I was not completely trusting of Cutting Edge, but I am never completely trusting of anybody. The Home Office replied to me saying recording equipment was allowed for prisoner's personal use, but not for entrapment.

On June 11 I again went to London. It was an unpleasant journey on a packed train from Holyhead, and a screaming young child added to the fun. I was reading the book ALL ABOUT JILL by David James Smith. Waiting on the platform in Oxford Circus Station I noticed a blonde woman with her back to me wearing a coat similar to what Jill Dando was wearing when she died. The woman held a large bunch of flowers and I felt uneasy as she very slowly turned around. Her face did not look at all like Jill's but she gave me the creeps. I put it down to the book I was reading.

Barry was again growing the awful beard and again he had no shoelaces. He was being punished so our visit was cut to one hour. Collective punishment I thought. When Margaret went to get tea I seized the opportunity and asked him 'did you ever meet Jill Dando?' He spread his arms and turned the palms of his hands up saying 'the only person I knew on that road was the doctor'. I would have preferred it if he had simply said no but that is the way he answers questions. One often has to try and interpret his answers. Margaret returned and the subject was immediately dropped.

I suggested that a suit would look good for the appeal, and said that I could help with that. As is typical with Barry he didn't really pay attention to what I was saying, and he went on to another topic which he wanted to speak about.

That evening there was a fire at Buckingham Palace. Fortunately it was quickly brought under control. The Golden Jubilee celebrations were in full swing and on bank holiday Monday the group Queen played their music from the roof of the palace.

On the following Friday David James Smith was interviewed on RTE's Marian Finucane's radio programme. He said Barry would probably lose his upcoming appeal and I had to agree with him. On Monday 10 I sent David Perrin copies of my photos of Barry.

I became ill a week later and was sick for the rest of June spending a few days in hospital. Not a pleasant experience though I did have a private room. I visited London while recovering and bought my first mobile phone.

David Perrin again asked me to give an interview but Margaret asked me not to. I decided to maintain a low profile for the long haul, if necessary.

Moneypenny phoned me on the June 20 saying there was a News of the World article claiming that Barry had stashed a pile of drugs. She acknowledged that she was wrong to have involved that paper. Fair play to her I thought, to admit a mistake.

Appeal

2002

One day in early July an angry Paddy Hill told me that he was finished supporting Barry, but later Moneypenny phoned to say that MOJO would still support him.

I returned to work on Friday 5 and within the first ten minutes my vehicle lights were broken by Hurley wielding thugs. It was back to normal for me on the mean streets of Limerick.

The following day Margaret told me that Barry wanted a suit for his appeal. But it was too late as the appeal was just a week away. He had to wear the clothes Margaret and Michelle provided, and he was rather cruelly described by the press as being dressed like a schoolboy.

Great Train Robber Ronnie Biggs got married the following week to his son Michael's mother in Belmarsh prison. I wrote to Barry saying that if things did not work out for him he should not give up hope, as we would continue to back him.

On Sunday 14 I visited Margaret, shortly before Michelle was expected to arrive. But some MOJO people met her at Heathrow Airport and a car took her straight to HMP Belmarsh, where Barry had been moved for the duration of his appeal.

When she finally arrived at Margaret's I advised her against making any statements during the period of the appeal but she dismissed my views saying 'I am a White City woman; his sister, I am entitled to speak out'. White City referred to the housing estate where she grew up. That evening she was shown on the TV news, as she walked to the doors of the prison to hand in the clothes for Barry's appeal.

The following morning as I prepared to go to the court she was on GMTV discussing the appeal. I thought that didn't seem right, and I decided then to avoid a planned united family entrance into the court, instead arriving alone at about 11.00. The hearing was in progress and I sat alongside Michelle, Margaret and Moneypenny. Dr Susan Young was also there. A representative of Kevin McNamara MP met me as I had asked a number of MPs to observe the appeal.

Barry was sat behind a twelve foot wrought iron railing, wearing a grey pullover and dark trousers.

In this description of the appeal I have drawn a little from my notes which are very general but in the interests of accuracy I have also drawn from the official judgement.

The Appeal was before The Lord Chief Justice of England & Wales (Lord Woolf) Mr Justice Curtis and Mister Justice Henriques.

Michael Mansfield QC and Maryam Syed for the appellant, (Barry) instructed by solicitor Marilyn Etienne.

Orlando Pownall and Jonathan Laidlaw for the Respondent. (Crown)

The grounds of appeal.

The appeal was based on the quality of identification and scientific evidence, abuse of process, i.e. adverse publicity when reporting restrictions were lifted, and the delay by the police in seeking to interview Barry. They had received information relating to him between 26 April 1999 and 14 June 1999. The steps taken to trace and interview him between February and May 2000 should have been taken as a matter of urgency it was claimed, between April and June 1999.

I had been under the misapprehension that the appeal judges would examine all the evidence that had been presented to the jury and in effect decide again. But that is not how it goes and I soon realised that this would be a hard fought appeal as the LCJ (Woolf) interrupted Mansfield on seemingly trivial details. At times Mansfield and Woolf seemed like old pals as they joked about a mysterious bunch of bananas. Woolf did not come across as the frighteningly stern looking old man he appeared to be in the Daily Mail's photographs; instead he seemed like quite a jolly old chap.

Abuse of process.

Mansfield had made an application in line with S.78 of PACE that the prosecution should have been stayed on the grounds of abuse of process due to the prejudice caused to Barry due to the delay in him being prosecuted, and the adverse publicity he received when Mr Justice Gage lifted the reporting restrictions. Gage dismissed that application. Mansfield contested that that decision was wrong. He claimed that the evidence as a whole showed that the conviction was unsafe, that there was a 'lurking doubt'. Barry had come to the attention of the police between April 26 1999 and June 14 1999 and the police waited until the following February before seeking to interview him. There was said Mansfield a breakdown of the system. As a result of the delay Barry was prejudiced in three ways, as to his alibi, the forensic evidence and the identification evidence.

The passage of time could have given the prosecution an advantage e.g. by claiming that Barry had time to dispose of evidence, and for people's memories to fade.

PACE = Police and Criminal Evidence (Act). Section 78 relates to the exclusion of unfair evidence. A trial judge has discretion whether to allow relevant evidence having regard to all the circumstances including how the evidence was obtained.

Identification.

Mansfield argued that safeguards built up over 1000 years were being thrown out. He pointed out that out of 9 witnesses only Susan Mayes had made an unqualified identification at the ID parade. All the other evidence of what occurred at the ID parades should have been excluded in line with S. 78 of PACE.

He argued that the evidence of those who failed to identify Barry should have been excluded, such as confusion caused by Barry's beard, or picking number 8 who looked like number 2, Barry. The only evidence that should be allowed in such cases he argued was that the witness had failed to make a positive identification.

Pownall argued that if the evidence was relevant and passed the quality test set by S.78 the judge should admit it, otherwise a witness who might be 90% sure or who under cross examination dropped from 100% sure to 95% would then be excluded.

There was, Pownall claimed, an underlying unity of description not only in descriptions but in the circumstances of what each witness saw the man doing. It was inconceivable that there were two men of similar appearance behaving in a similar manner in Gowan Avenue so close to the time of the murder.

The jury issue.

After the trial had ended one upset juror attempted to contact Barry's solicitor. It was not publicly known if it was the male juror who had voted not guilty.

However in an unfortunate slip of the tongue Mansfield referred to the juror as 'she'. He apologised immediately for his mistake. Due to rules surrounding juries there was little that could be done on that issue. (But as a result of the slip of the tongue we now knew that there was a second juror who disagreed with the verdict. Very strange.)

John McVicar's book DEAD on TIME was referred to as it appeared to claim that some impropriety had taken place involving unauthorised conversations with jurors. On April 30 Lord Woolf, Lord Justice Mantell and Mr Justice Leveson had heard an application on that matter. No inquiry was ordered but it was indicated that the police could make appropriate inquiries if they saw fit.

Forensics

The main aspect of the scientific evidence related to guns and the issue of innocent contamination. Mansfield submitted that Mr Justice Gage was wrong in not agreeing to the submission of no case to answer in as far as the FDR evidence related to the identification and/or was wrong in directing the jury that the FDR residue was capable of providing support for the identification.

At lunchtime we went across the road from the court to the George pub but I could not get a cup of tea. Paddy Hill then arrived followed by a camera crew. I left and went up Fleet Street where I managed to get some tea. 'This is turning into another bloody media circus', I thought.

On the news that evening I watched Michelle's morning statement on the steps of the court as she attacked what she claimed British Justice had done to her family over the past year. It was an impressive performance and she looked and sounded good while Margaret remained completely silent. I wondered if the appeal judges were impressed by it all. Another relative tried to reassure me that the judges were above being influenced by such things. I was not convinced; judges are human, aren't they?

The appeal hearing ended earlier than expected on Tuesday, and judgement was reserved. Mansfield gathered his bits and pieces and prepared to leave the building. I spoke with him briefly about the media statements and interviews. He did not seem to be very happy. I never met him again but I sought his advice on some matters in later years and he was good enough to give it.

Again there was a big statement made to the TV cameras outside the Law Courts. I kept to one side out of camera view as Margaret and Michelle were filmed getting into the posh looking car which was laid on by Cutting Edge. I slipped away up Kingsway to Holborn Tube Station.

On my way home on Saturday 20 I bought the Irish Independent. Michelle was featured in an article by Justine McCarthy. There was a glowing account of her support for Barry and a reference to an Irish uncle who had recently sent Barry some money to buy chocolate and phone cards.

In fact Barry did use most of his money on overpriced prison phone cards to phone his mother and solicitor, and though I would send him a little money from time to time it was his mother who made regular contributions to him.

Michelle and Margaret visited Barry on Monday and Michelle told me that he was anxious about his appeal prospects. Good I thought, don't get your hopes up.

Jeffrey Archer lost his appeal against conviction and perjury on July 22. The courts findings were read out in two minutes. Lady Archer had kept a dignified silence during the appeal, but let rip brilliantly on the steps of the court *after* the appeal was dismissed.

The appeal judges gave their findings on Barry's appeal on Monday July 29. This time I was again staying with Margaret. On the Sunday London sweltered in 30 degrees of heat. In the evening Michelle Moneypenny and Paddy Hill arrived in East Acton along with the Cutting Edge team. There seemed to be big plans in place for Barry if he was released. I became concerned about what might happen and I wrote a letter to him with some advice.

I declined the offer of a drive to court for the appeal findings, taking the Tube instead. I had breakfast in Fleet Street and then entered the court early. I gave Marilyn Etienne the letter for Barry and I thought she looked a little sad. She advised me to secure our seats, as Michelle and Margaret were late as their car was stuck in traffic. Fortunately Barry's prison van was also delayed so nobody noticed their late arrival.

The court was packed. The judges came in, but there was no sign of Mansfield. Instead a little foot stool was on his table. We asked Etienne where he was and she seemed a little embarrassed as she said 'He isn't here'.

Copies of the courts findings were given out to the press and Moneypenny got one. She handed it to me pointing to four words, 'We dismiss this appeal'. I walked out in disgust a few minutes later having no intention of sitting listening to what I considered to be a whitewash.

It took two hours for the judges to read out their findings. These were basically that the trial judge Mr Justice Gage had acted properly in his conclusions and decisions during the course of the trial. They appeared if anything to have strengthened the case against Barry. E.g. they found that the single polyester fibre though weak evidence nevertheless showed a two way contact between Barry and Jill Dando. They said he had a Kalashnikov when in fact he had a plastic replica machine gun.

The LCJ summed up the 60 page judgement: 'Looking at the evidence as a whole we have no doubt as to the correctness of the conviction.'

The defence then announced that they would seek permission to appeal to the House of Lords on a point of law.

*

This is an account of the official Appeal Court summary.

No one saw this murder which was committed on 26 April 1999. The murderer escaped: the firearm he used was never found.

The investigation was complex and difficult.

The Appeal Court after a full review has decided, as the Trial Judge did, that the delay in arresting this Appellant was understandable and that it did not compromise his defence or alibi, nor his case that many witnesses did not identify him on the video parade. The prosecution did not rely on the delay in any way unfair to the Appellant so as to require the Judge to use his power to rule out the evidence in fact, given to him under his powers to exclude "unfair evidence' (under S 78 Police and Criminal Evidence Act 1984). There was no abuse of the process of Law.

The complaint by the Appellant about the lurid headlines and numerous photographs with unfortunate comments about the Appellant in sections of the media following the Judge's lifting of the ban against publication of such material on 28 February 2000 is highly regrettable but it did not in the Court's view prevent a fair trial. The trial Judge was not to know at the time of the lifting of the ban that such lack of restraint would be shown.

Identification

The Appellant's main argument was that only clear and unqualified identifications should be permitted in evidence. In this case there are three relevant points:-

(i) The gap in time between the murder and the identifications —viz April 1999 to August or October 2000.

(ii) The Appellant refused to stand on any parade after the first one. The police had to resort to the less satisfactory video "parade" when those in the video-photographs wore beards as the Appellant did late in the year 2000, but did not wear at the time of sightings in 1999.

(iii) It is conceded by the Defence that one witness did make an unqualified identification from which the jury could conclude he was the murderer.

The Appeal Court rejects the Defence argument.

In addition to the unqualified identification there was a pattern of evidence from some nine witnesses describing a man and describing his actions, which considered as a whole showed a consistency of evidence that there cannot have been two men of that description and behaviour as described in the area local to the Appellant and his victim.

Other evidence supported the Prosecution's case:

1. The finding of a particle of firearm discharge residue found in the Appellant's coat, itself unusual in persons not associated with firearms and in the light of most of the residue having gone into the victim's head which was consistent with it having come from the firing of the cartridge found at the scene. The Court considers the jury were fully entitled to reject the evidence that the coat had been innocently contaminated and accept contrary evidence that this was not so.

2. The finding of a fibre on the victim consistent with having come from the Appellant's clothing which though weak in itself, in association with the other evidence, showed a two-way link connection by forensic evidence between the Appellant and the victim.

3. The fact that the Appellant was despite his untrue denials associated with firearms. For example, the police found a photograph of him in military combat clothing holding a gun not dissimilar from the murder weapon.

4. The fact that the Appellant showed an obsession with Miss Dando and other female television Presenters as shown by his collection of photographs and the like found by the police at his home.

5. The lies he told police when questioned.

6. The flawed alibi statement by the Appellant from which it could be properly deduced he tried after the murder to say he was at HAFAD or a taxi firm's office at the time of the killing.

There was no evidence from the Appellant to contradict or explain any of this evidence or the deductions which could properly be drawn from it.

Circumstantial evidence is not second-class evidence but it requires and has received careful analysis. In this case the whole picture presented by the evidence is, in the opinion of this court, compelling and the conviction was correct.

———————————————

I was a little concerned about how Barry would react, but I later discovered that he was informed of the findings before the start.

Margaret was shattered though she did not collapse as was reported. I think we all felt as if all hope had died there. We had naively thought that Barry was convicted by a jury which was confused by all the evidence, but that the appeal court being made up of learned judges would see that the conviction was clearly wrong and overturn it. It was the blackest period for us.

The BBC's Jeremy Britton met me outside the courtroom and asked me if there would be a statement. I was still shocked at the findings, and passed him on to Moneypenny. We were asked to wait in the court cafeteria until Maryam Syed and Marilyn Etienne had spoken to Barry.

We left the building at 13.30. I remained inside the doorway for a while chatting with Dr Susan Young while Michelle read a statement prepared by the defence team for Barry. 'I have spent over two years in prison for a crime I simply did not commit. I have struggled hard during this prosecution against me to keep my faith in the British justice system. Today that faith and belief has been destroyed'.

Marilyn Etienne said that the judges had changed the 'rules and safeguards enshrined in our system in order to protect innocent people from wrongful conviction'. Hamish Campbell said 'A compelling case was placed before the jury and they found Barry George guilty of murder. Their verdict has been shown to be a proper one and I consider the judgement of the Court of Appeal is the right decision'.

I hoped to slip quietly away, but Moneypenny nabbed me and persuaded me to go along to a news conference in a Hotel near Kings Cross. I went along but declined to join in, instead opting to have some more tea. I was sickened by it all, the game played out in the courtroom and the media antics played outside. Barry I felt was only a pawn in their game.

Later in the evening we had a drink with David Perrin and James Cohen. We managed to persuade Michelle not to take part in a late night talk radio show. David threw a chilling example of a question she might face if she took part. That decided the matter for Michelle and she took Margaret home.

Later I became a little disturbed by something that James said. He asked me what I thought of the madness in the family. Fortunately Moneypenny had said to me earlier that James and David would get me drunk so I was on guard and drank very little. I asked him to define what he meant by madness. David then interrupted and the young production manager distracted me with conversation, but I could not miss a quiet but furious argument between David and James. It made me think that the Cutting Edge programme could go either way, either promoting Barry's innocence or guilt.

I got back to East Acton about 22.30 and had a relaxing pint on my own. Having had no dinner I got a takeaway chicken and chips and went back to the house. I kept very quiet and did not turn on the TV as Margaret and Michelle were gone to bed. But before I could finish my meal Margaret came downstairs, and stood silently waiting until I went to my room. I often wondered who the real prisoner was. I could not sleep what with trying to digest the awful appeal result, a bellyful of barely eaten chicken, and the stifling London heat. A car arrived about 05.30 to take Michelle to another TV interview with GMTV. She was going to be interviewed along with the writer Don Hale, author of the book Town Without Pity.

I turned on the TV to see GMTV at 06.00. Michelle and Don were being interviewed. Michelle was speaking and suddenly departed from the agreed script. She made serious allegations which for legal reasons I can't repeat but I had to laugh as the male interviewer vainly tried to stop her on live TV. The allegation was not repeated or broadcast again but it was made nevertheless. I left the house at 07.30 and went home.

The press had a field day. NO DOUBT the tabloid headlines screamed. It felt like the final defeat and I felt I had to reply.

Letter to the Daily Mirror.

31-7-2002'

Dear Sir/Madam

Voice of the Daily Mirror, 30-7-2002 has echoes of Denning's 'Appalling Vista' about it. Barry George's appeal verdict was a sad day for justice. But it will not end there.

M. Burke.
Mike Burke.

Being a glutton for punishment on the following Saturday I was once again on the train going back to take Margaret to visit Barry.

I was a little surprised at Holyhead station to see a policeman wearing a flak jacket looking out at me from the ticket office as I bought my train ticket. I bought a Cornish pasty and a cup of tea before boarding the train. I was reading a new book by Ludovic Kennedy, 'Thirty Six-Murders & Two Immoral Earnings'. As the train made its way across Anglesey Island I noticed that my carriages lights were not working. As we approached Bangor we went into a tunnel and it all went black. Then I noticed the same policeman making his way back from the front of the train towards me. I thought of the allegation Michelle had made and felt a little uneasy. I slipped the book under my seat. The policeman did not speak to me, but as the train waited at Bangor Station he stood on the platform alongside my window. I am sure he had no interest in me, but it made me think that what Michelle had said was not very wise. She was safely at home in Cork, while my family had to live in London, and I would be travelling over and back alone for the foreseeable future. My memories of the '70s and '80s and the Prevention of Terrorism Act came to mind. Fellows travelling alone could very easily come a cropper. Anybody who thinks I was unnecessarily paranoid should read up on the McGuire Seven and Giuseppe Conlon cases.

However in the next six years I never again saw a policeman in the ticket office or on the train, nor did I ever have any hassle with police.

On Sunday August 4 as Margaret and I waited at Kings Cross station I bought the Sunday Mirror. There was a photo of Margaret which she did not like as she looked very angry. Also there was one of my photos of Barry with his two sisters, Susan and Michelle, which I had taken at Michelle's wedding reception at Cork's Blackrock Castle in 1982. Margaret was quoted in the paper as saying that Barry might have been cleared if only he had taken on Gareth Peirce. I foolishly said that it might have been better if that had not been reported, and so Margaret was angry with me for the rest of the day.

Rain lashed the ground at March Station as we ran to the taxi office. It was hot and wet and our nerves were frayed.

'Barry, I have to ask you something' I said as Margaret got the tea. 'Did you do it?'

He didn't get angry or hit me as I feared, but just wearily shook his head and quietly said 'No, I didn't'. He then told me that he had sacked his defence team. He was puzzled and upset that Mansfield had not been present when the appeal court gave their findings. I asked him about the photo of him with the gas mask and gun, and he said that he had hoped to use that as publicity for his hoped for work as a stuntman and the gun which the appeal court said was a Kalashnikov was in fact a plastic toy or replica. He complained that he had nothing to do, no study or work, just pool and TV, and not enough exercise.

At Peterborough station I got a cup of tea and a sandwich in the cafeteria. The young female cashier was star struck as she said to me 'I've just seen Ann Widdecombe'. (Tory MP) I laughed as I said 'you never know who you are talking to'.

We got the delayed 16.52 train at 16.57 back to Kings Cross. Just a few miles away in Soham Village the terrible tragedy of Holly Well's and Jessica Chapman was unfolding. School caretaker Ian Huntley would later be convicted of their murders.

On Monday 19 the Cutting Edge programme went out on Channel 4. The programme was very positive, and featured my photos of Barry, the same photos which caused all the trouble. Barry's former Fulham neighbours cast doubt on his ability to have carried out the murder, and the programme questioned the timings of the events as put forward by the Crown. According to Cutting Edge 'the times simply do not add up'. I was a little puzzled at the use of medical evidence on the programme which was said to be used 'with permission'. Who would have given permission? I wondered, as Barry is very sensitive about his health issues. I later made some discreet inquiries and was given the name. Barry was quite angry that his health issues were aired and he protested that he had not given his permission.

He was now without a solicitor, though Marilyn Etienne would be on board for the House of Lords appeal. We were hoping that Gareth Peirce would then be able to take up his case, despite being up to her eyes in work due to the fall out from 9-11.

I heard through the grapevine that MOJO / Michelle were going to make a submission to the CCRC on Barry's behalf. I was a little concerned as I felt it should be done with Barry's cooperation by his solicitor. I contacted both MOJO and Michelle asking them to hold on and let Gareth Peirce do it after Marilyn Etienne took the point of law to the House of Lords but on the Sunday Mirror of September 29 there was a report that a submission was about to be made. The report disclosed details of the contents of the submission. As a result I then sent the CCRC some information including Home Office advice which I thought might help Barry, but I would have preferred if the submission's had been made by a qualified solicitor. Unfortunately most submissions not prepared by a suitably qualified solicitor are doomed to failure. In a few years his lawyers would make another submission.

Relations between some members of my own Family became strained as most felt that as Barry was convicted and had appealed we should leave it at that. But I was convinced that the conviction was unsafe. I accepted that there was a possibility that Barry was the man, but the evidence used to convict him was unconvincing. To the best of my knowledge Barry had no interest in Jill Dando prior to her murder. There is no denying that he had an interest after her murder, but that is typical of him.

One day I got a text message from Michelle, saying that a singer songwriter from West Sussex, Martin Jeremiah had written a song about Barry, called 'Dragon Slew George'.

In late September I began compiling material for a website, checking dates and facts and trying to tie them all together, writing and tearing up and starting again.

On October 13 the Sunday Mirror published an article by Don Hale giving an account of a visit with Paddy Hill to see Barry. It was titled

'The First Prison Interview' and cast very serious doubt on Barry's ability to be the cool calculating hit man.

I thought it was a very good article, but Barry was furious as he believed he had been portrayed as a bumbling idiot. Barry can be very unforgiving and so he would never let Paddy or Don visit him again. I could appreciate how he felt even though I thought it was a very positive article.

In late October I sent a strongly worded letter to MOJO complaining about their tactics. By now the website was taking shape, and I was involved in a struggle as to what direction it should take. The webmaster Mick Lynch wanted to portray Barry as innocent, but I insisted that we should question the safety of the conviction, rather than call it a Miscarriage of Justice. I wanted people to judge for themselves and in the end I won out.

On Tuesday November 5 I was tempted to run from East Acton station to Margaret's as rockets and bangers exploded all around the place. It was Guy Fawkes Day, and it felt like a battle zone. Michelle was in Birmingham with MOJO presenting their submission to the CCRC. Margaret and I met her in HMP Whitemoor the next day. Barry was very upset with Michelle because of press reports and the CCRC submission. He said that it should have been left to his solicitor to make the submission, and he feared that his prospects might now have been damaged. He said that he thought the visit by Don Hale and Paddy Hill was a private visit and he felt betrayed that it had been reported. It was a difficult visit where Barry threatened to have Michelle jailed if she did not respect his views. He no longer wanted MOJO to be involved in his situation. In time he would threaten to have us all jailed, which probably was a reflection of his frustration at not being in control of the things which concerned him.

That evening I met David Perrin in a Shepherds Bush pub where we had a nice pint of Guinness. We discussed the website and he gave me some advice on that saying that I should look at Susan May's website. He then said that Barry's supporters seemed to be fragmented, and suggested that it would be more effective if there was a combined united push for Barry. Good advice I thought.

On Thursday Michelle and Margaret took Sheba the cat to the vet, as she had a sore mouth. In the evening I told Michelle about the planned website, and about David's suggestion of a united front. She did not seem to be very interested. Later Hazel Keirle from MOJO phoned Michelle to make arrangements for Michelle's next TV appearance, on SKY News. Michelle wanted them to show the videotape which I had loaned her, showing the man who was supposed to be Barry at Princess Diana's vigil. She wanted to show how inaccurate identification can be.

I returned home next day and the news was all about a terror alert on a British car ferry. Very reassuring I thought as I crossed the Irish Sea on the Stena fast ferry. That night I watched Michelle's SKY News interview and I was shocked at her appearance. She looked pale and strained and the interviewer did not give her a soft interview. They did not use the video of the man in the park as Michelle had wanted.

On Sunday we had agreed on the first page of the website. I wrote to MOJO suggesting that we should form a united campaign front for Barry. The 'site was up and running on November 20. <u>www.barrygeorge.co.uk</u>

'He's Net Guilty', the Irish Mirror reported, next to a large photo of Michelle and Margaret. The Guardian also gave it a mention in an article on prisoner websites.

MOJO's Hazel Keirle wrote to me, saying that MOJO was not in any way a campaign group, but she advised that I could form a campaign. So with the help of the webmaster Mick Lynch I contacted the 'Irish In Britain Representation Group' or the IBRG to see if they would help.

I went to London on December 12 and met Pat Reynolds, the IBRG Chairman, at Margaret's house. We discussed a campaign plan, and agreed to think things over. Pat then spoke to Michelle on the phone, but she was now tied up with MOJO and told Pat that Barry already had their support. The campaign was hampered from the word go but I was determined to push ahead and managed to persuade Pat to remain on board.

Margaret and I made our Christmas visit to Barry on Saturday December 14. The visit was cut to just over one hour. The Christmas presents of a jumper and shoes which Margaret had sent him were returned to her by the prison, without any explanation. He was surprisingly upbeat, despite the recent ruling that his case could not go to the House of Lords. He asked me to contact Marilyn Etienne and ask her to hand over his court papers to his new solicitor, Gareth Peirce.

Incidentally, Margaret gave me the shoes which fitted my size 11 feet perfectly.

PART 2

J f B

2003

In July 2001 Barry George was convicted of the murder of BBC TV presenter Jill Dando. In July 2002 he lost his appeal and was now consigned to spend the rest of his life in HM Prison. However he still denied being responsible for the murder and his family had vowed to battle on to try and clear his name. Though a rift between his supporters had opened by the end of 2002 the fight back had begun.

*

On January 25 2003 the Justice for Barry or JfB campaign emerged. There was no fanfare but I knew that Barry and his mother were in favour of it and that was the relevant test.

JfB was always a small loosely knit group and we did not normally seek or encourage people to join us, though we sought support for the cause. We feared police or journalist infiltration, and I would point to the group MOJO as justification of that caution. I believe that if the campaign rather than Barry had become the focus of attention it would not have stood the test of time, and we were in it for the long haul, in good times and bad. Mostly bad.

We requested that the Home Secretary would review Barry's Cat 'A' status, and that he be moved to a London prison to help his mother make her regular visits.

While we were working on the website on February 1 Mick's partner Joy got an e-mail from America telling her that the space shuttle Columbia had just exploded. I later sent eight letters to various MP's seeking support.

On Saturday 15 there was a huge demonstration in London, protesting at the looming war in Iraq.

I designed a leaflet and Mick made up a prototype which I then got printed. The leaflet described Barry as a proud Englishman with Welsh Irish roots. He was described as not a devil, not a saint, but perhaps a Scapegoat. It then pointed to some shortcomings of the jury, and there followed a description of the case against Barry, and the scant forensic evidence. It also contained a list of people who felt or expressed CONCERN at the safety of Barry's conviction. Eventually I had a short list, small in number but impressive in quality.

The list consisted of Willie O Dea, TD. John McDonnell, MP. Professor Tim Valentine. Jim Nichol, Solicitor. John Witzenfeld. Solicitor. Pat Reynolds, Chairman IBRG. Dr Chris R Tame, Director Libertarian Alliance. Billy Power and Paddy Hill. (Birmingham Six) Andy Parr. (Cricket writer) Paul Foot, Journalist. Later I would get a few more names. They were Jeremy Corbyn, MP. John McManus, MOJO. LA Naylor, author of HOW MANY ARE INNOCENT. Senator Labhras O Murchu. Professor Elizabeth Loftus, 'Memory expert' who was concerned at witnesses recollections. Seamus Healy TD. Dan Neville TD. The leaflet ended with information on our website and a request for concerned people to write to their local politician or MEP, and a mention of Martin Jeremiah and his album Day Off For The Queen.

I planned to distribute some at the London Saint Patrick's Day Festival in March. I also sent some to politicians, the Home Office etc. Michelle phoned to tell me that she would also be in London, as MOJO were holding a public meeting in the House of Commons. I was not invited which I thought was a pity as we could perhaps have distributed some more of the leaflets.

When we visited Barry on the Saturday the atmosphere in the visitor's hall was oppressive. A female officer seemed resentful, and watched us closely. At one point Michelle's foot was in contact with the horizontal bar of a seat, touching it but not on it, and the female officer sent a young male officer to tell Michelle to move her foot. It was petty, almost like being back in Belmarsh.

Michelle left for home early on Sunday morning, and I went to the South Bank where a policeman helped me with directions in locating the IBRG stall. Pat Reynolds and Andy Parr were there, along with Mick Gilgunn of the trade union UCATT. The family of the jailed young Irish jockey Christy McGrath were also present. Christy had pleaded guilty to killing the former footballer Gary Walton in a brawl. After he had pleaded guilty the police revealed that Gary died from strangulation. Christy denied strangling Gary, but it was too late due to the guilty plea. So Christy could not appeal his conviction.

It was a beautiful sunny day. We distributed leaflets and collected signatures for a petition. One young man sought me out by name due to the website and told me that he also believed that Barry was innocent.

On April 11 I wrote to the Director General of the BBC, Greg Dyke, accusing the BBC of allowing itself to be manipulated by Hamish Campbell's Crimewatch UK appearance. In the programme Hamish and Nick Ross had discussed the profile of the type of person who might have killed Jill Dando. The profile was remarkably similar to Barry's, but he was already being investigated by Hamish and I suspected that Ross knew that. I felt it was a cynical grooming of TV viewers prior to arrest.

The BBC replied, saying that Crimewatch UK was made in close co-operation with the police. They suggested that Barry's solicitor might like to discuss the matter with their legal department. I passed the reply to solicitor Gareth Peirce but heard no more about it.

I next drove to London on the day the war in Iraq officially ended, April 9. 'Hostilities over', declared George Bush. Some Iraqi's obviously thought differently and Iraq would dominate the news, for the rest of the decade and more.

Air force aircraft roared over the prison the next day as Barry asked us to get an injunction to stop the upcoming TV programme 'The Hunt for Jill Dando's Killer'. He thought that if only he could appear in court the judge would then realise that he should not be in prison, and his release would be ordered. 'Dream on' I thought, but I passed on his request to Gareth Peirce who confirmed that it would not be possible. While on a few days sick leave following an assault at work I watched the Channel 4 programme as Barry was shown allegedly lying. That was when the police asked him who the man in the photo holding a broken gun and wearing a gas mask was. Barry said he didn't know, and took a second look when told that it was him in the photo. I believed when I was watching it that the police had developed the photo, so I did not think he told a lie when he did not immediately recognise himself. He clearly denied killing Jill Dando on the police video. Some years later I read that the police had found the negative, and if true then it would seem that Barry should have known it was him in the photo.

On Thursday May 15 I went to a meeting in Dublin at Leinster House. It was for to raise awareness of the plight of Christy McGrath

The McGrath family were there, along with Pat Reynolds, Andy Parr and Mick Gilgunn. 'Where is Michelle?' Mick asked, surprised at her absence. I had invited her but she couldn't make it due to work commitments.

We met many T.D's and a few ministers. The McGrath family got lots of promises and some sound advice. Barry got the support of two more TDs, Seamus Healy and Dan Neville, in addition to Willie O Dea who was then Irish Minister of State for Justice.

We made plans to mark the third anniversary of the arrest. Andy favoured a picket of Hammersmith police station, but eventually we decided on the Home Office.

On May 22 I bought my first computer, a Laptop Compaq, an excellent item which I used to write this book. Andy phoned that night to discuss the picket. Michelle also phoned wondering if MOJO would be welcome on the picket. I said ok, but that it might be best if Paddy Hill stayed away so as to avoid a clash with Andy. Paddy and Andy had had a falling out over Christy McGrath.

The train from Holyhead to London took eight and a half hours due to line disruption. I arrived at East Acton in time for a quick pint. Margaret and I visited Barry the next day, Sunday. He was in good spirits and the staff were friendly.

On Monday Margaret had to go to hospital for tests, but she said that she would still like to come along to the picket which was planned for the evening. I managed to dissuade her. I spent the afternoon making up placards, and I went to Saint James underground station arriving just before five thirty, as planned. There were about six policemen outside on the street. I walked around the area to get my bearings. At six thirty I was still alone, and then Pat Reynolds arrived, having been busy in court all day. Nobody else came, so we had a cup of tea in McDonalds, Victoria, and that was that. Quite embarrassing but an eye opener also. We decided then to forget about street demonstrations, thinking it would be best to conduct the campaign via the internet. It was suggested to us a few times over the next few years that we should have protest marches but we felt that it would be too difficult to organise and ensure any demonstrations passed off peacefully. So we maintained a low key campaign. Unfortunately we lacked a figurehead, a Face for the campaign.

Why nobody else came to the planned demonstration I don't know. But I do know that peoples careers can suffer if they challenge the establishment and that may have been the reason. By forming the JfB campaign we were in effect challenging the system, the established order. That has its dangers and the dark forces of the establishment can hit back. Some years later a son of Pat Reynolds would be wrongly targeted in relation to a high profile murder case.

In early July the Home Office wrote to me addressing all the points we had made on the JfB leaflet.

The big news now was the strange death of Doctor David Kelly, the government scientist who allegedly killed himself, though some think that he may have been murdered. Doctor Kelly was the source behind a BBC claim that the UK government had 'sexed up' the case for war in Iraq.

Mike Burke

When Margaret and I visited Barry on July 20 he was very uptight. He was angry with Michelle, MOJO, the Sunday Mirror and Gareth Peirce. He threatened to sack Peirce. It was a difficult and unpleasant visit. Following an earlier request a friendly young female officer took a photo of Margaret, Barry and I. That photo would later cause quite a fuss. Jeffrey Archer was released from prison the next day, which I watched on Sky News as I travelled home. I was quite pleased that he was freed having enjoyed reading his book FF8282.

On August 1 I received a letter from a student and campaigner from Derby, Scott Lomax.

I tried to take advantage of the August Silly Season to try and get an article published, but to no avail. The press interest seemed to have gone.

The Home Office wrote to me again informing me that Barry's Cat 'A' status would be reviewed in the New Year, and that a judge would set a Tariff for Barry sometime after November. They never did set one and I came to believe that he would have to serve a full life tariff if we failed to get him out. By 'we' I mean *all* his supporters and legal teams.

As the year wore on I continued sending JfB leaflets to MP's including Tony Blair, Michael Howard, and Gerry Adams.

On December 2 I heard that Barry had a new solicitor, Jeremy Moore from Manchester. On Friday 12 Margaret and I visited Barry who confirmed that Gareth Peirce was now off his case. On Sunday it was reported 'We Got Him' as Saddam Hussein was captured.

On Monday I met Andy Parr for another visit to the House of Commons where we met with MP Jeremy Corbyn. Andy pointed out a brass plaque where King Charles I faced his final court.

On Boxing Day another awful murder occurred in Leeds. Traffic policeman PC Ian Broadhurst arrested a suspicious motorist but when he tried to handcuff him the motorist pulled a gun shooting PC Broadhurst and two colleagues. The motorist, Nathan Wayne Coleman finished Ian off as he lay injured on the ground. Coleman fled the scene.

On New Year's Eve Coleman was arrested by armed police in a hotel room. He had the murder weapon and 200 rounds of ammunition under his pillow, but surrendered in order to survive.

The Croatian gun used to shoot the policemen is said to have come from a consignment of weapons which went missing during the Yugoslavian wars. Many such guns are said to have been linked to bank robberies and killings across Europe.

Nathan Coleman turned out to be fugitive David Bieber, an ex US Marine who was wanted in Florida for first degree murder since 1995. He is said to have paid a hitman $1000 to shoot bodybuilder Markus Mueller, a love rival who was shot on his doorstep. Bieber is also linked to the shooting of his ex-girlfriend.

A search of a lock up near Bieber's home in Leeds revealed bullet making equipment and the police suspected it was linked to Bieber.

Could there be a link to the Dando murder we wondered? We studied the case but in the end it seemed unlikely that there was any connection. We would however watch other cases over the following years to see if there were any connections or similarities.

Tolpuddle

2004

In January 2004 a letter arrived at JfB's London address from a man who claimed to have knowledge of who was really behind Jill Dando's murder. We advised him that if he had relevant information then he should contact the police and or Barry's solicitor. I understand that the same man later confessed to Hamish Campbell that he had killed Jill Dando but he could not corroborate his claim and was dismissed as just another attention seeker. He is probably innocent of the Dando murder but he is not an entirely innocent or harmless individual and he seems to take pleasure in issuing threats. There was later an allegation that the man had tried to blackmail Jill and shot her when she refused to pay up, but that may be just another fantasy.

I was also in touch through Andy Parr with the journalist Bob Woffinden, who had written an excellent article on the case called 'A shadow of doubt'. I hoped he might do another article to mark the fifth anniversary of the murder, which might lead to John McDonnell MP raising an Early Day Motion in Parliament.

In early February Margaret told me that a priest attached to the Irish embassy in London had visited Barry. I had written to the priest requesting that he visit and Barry was pleased that he had.

On Thursday 26 I met Andy Parr and Bob Woffinden in a nice little coffee shop in Piccadilly, opposite Starbucks. We had a good chat. Bob was still very much interested in the Serb theory, which Andy disagreed with. I ran an alternative theory past Bob but he didn't buy it. As we said goodbye I noticed that he gave me an odd look, and I think he probably thought that I was just another nutter. I didn't hear from him again until 2007.

The next day Margaret and I visited Barry. It was a routine visit, uneventful expect for our bad moods.

I was in Tralee on Thursday March 11 and I watched the Sky News reports on the Madrid train bombing which killed 170 and injured many more. The next day I was on the train again going to London for the London Saint Patrick's Day Festival. We visited Barry on Saturday.

Sunday was rather wet and windy. In the morning I met David James Smith in Mario's café in East Acton. We had a good chat and David shared many of my doubts surrounding Barry's conviction.

However he felt that Barry was guilty as he had spoken with Hamish Campbell and found him to be convincing.

I went to the Festival where I met Andy and Pat Reynolds at the IBRG stall. Simon Hughes MP took a JfB leaflet and in answer to the question on the leaflet 'Is his conviction safe?' said 'The answer to that is No'. Andy and I later bumped into John McDonnell MP as we walked towards Westminster Bridge. The bridge area resembled a war zone with roadside barriers in place to prevent an attack on the House of Commons.

At the end of March Hamish Campbell had a successful end to the 1997 Katerina Koneva murder case which I referred to in Operation Oxborough. Fingerprints were found on a window which her killer escaped through, and a single hair was found on Katerina's cardigan. Eventually those clues led police to her killer, a Polish sex offender, Andrezej Kunowski. He had 27 previous convictions in Poland. In one case in 1995 he followed a schoolgirl home and when she opened her door he forced his way in and then raped her. He had attacked females ranging in age from 11 to 30. He arrived in the UK in 1996 under a false name and using a forged passport. He raped a 21 year old woman in his West London flat in 2002 and in 2003 he was sentenced to nine years in jail. He was later charged with Katerina's murder, found guilty and told that he would die in prison.

I had failed to persuade anyone to do a helpful article to mark the fifth anniversary of Jill Dando's murder, but to my surprise on April 25 the News of the World magazine did publish an excellent article.

On May 14 Margaret and a friend went to visit Barry, but when they arrived Margaret discovered that she had forgotten her visiting order and so she was not allowed in. I went over on Friday 21 and the next day we visited him. I asked him why he was arrested at Kensington Palace and he said that he had fallen asleep in the grounds as he made his way back from Chelsea barracks in 1983.

The next day was a beautiful sunny day and I went along to Kensington Palace armed with my new toy, a Canon *Power-shot A80* Digital camera. I walked around the palace and bought a couple of postcards. I noted all the bushes where one could hide, and also the high walls and security cameras. I doubted that Barry would have been silly enough to have contemplated breaking in, though Michael Fagin had set a precedent back in 1982 when he entered the Queens bedroom in Buckingham Palace and asked her for a cigarette. My only doubt in relation to Barry was that it was mid winter when he claimed to have gone for his sleep outside the palace, but maybe he thought it was endurance training for his SAS fantasy. I don't know.

The Case of Barry George by Scott Lomax was published on Thursday 27, and he sent me a signed copy. He argued the case for Barry's innocence well and I thought it was a very positive development. The book had a photo of Barry on the cover which I had lent to Scott with permission to use.

On June 26 the Daily Express did a two page spread on Scott's book. A couple of days later Michelle featured in an Irish evening paper, and appeared to dismiss the value of Scott's book, saying that a book would not get Barry out. I was disappointed at the dismissal of what was a very well argued case by a young writer who was supportive of Barry, who needed all the support he could get.

On July 17 I drove to Tolpuddle in Dorset for the Tolpuddle Martyrs Festival. I was very tired as I made my way up the M4 through Wales, but a nice cup of tea revived me. I crossed the Severn Bridge and branched off towards Bristol, heading south. Somewhere off to my right was Weston Super Mare, Jill Dando's birthplace.

Heavy rain lashed the roads as I drove along through the rolling hills and I wondered if Sunday would be a washout. It cleared as I drove into Dorset, and I made my way to the little village of Tolpuddle. I could not find anywhere to stay there as the trade unions had everyplace booked up, so I drove back to Dorchester where I booked into the Casterbridge Hotel. Later that night Tony Benn and his son Hillary also checked into the hotel but I did not have the pleasure of meeting them.

In the morning after an excellent full English breakfast I drove to the festival. 'Nice to see somebody from Limerick' said the man at the entrance to the field which acted as a car park. I made my way to the big marquee where Martin Jeremiah had a stand booked. I found his table where his partner Vicky had set up a display featuring JfB leaflets, the Scott Lomax book and some other material which I had sent on ahead, some of which alleged a 'Dando Cover Up'.

I almost missed Martin playing his song 'Dragon Slew George' from the main stage.

Now here's a fairy story, or so some people say,
Of the Jill Dando murder so
Someone they had to pay
But they had no murder weapon and no one at the scene
With theories of a gangland hit the chances they were lean.

They called in all the profilers and put George in the frame
The Yorkshire ripper taught them well
But they found George not to blame
Another year or so goes by and policemen are all through
The Dando hit-man trail still cold
So they say that George will do.

Chorus

And the dragon came breathing firey words
As the press they went to town
The scales of justice in his jaws
With one side weighted down
And Georgie Porgy pudding head spy
Said catch me coz you can
The dragon slayed poor Georgie
Coz he was no saintly man.
The police they took a powder speck
From a nut that liked toy guns
For playing with spent cartridges
They could have nicked my son
Fuelled by Georgies fantasies
They put him in his place

Discredited I.D. parades
Designed to fit his face

So what are we going to do about it?
Martin Jeremiah.

*

It was brilliant to hear the song live. When he had finished I introduced myself, and then I met Vicky. We went for a beer, excellent looking home made stuff but unfortunately I could not have any as I would be driving back to Dorchester later.

About mid day Martin gave a rendition of the trade union movement history through the ages featuring stories and songs. He described how the Cotton Mill workers slaved in the Mill's without adequate working conditions, and of how the six Tolpuddle Martyr's came to be deported to Australia in the early 1800s. Suddenly there was a power cut and Martin said 'That's the end of history as we know it'.

Later we took part in the Parade of Banners as the various trade unions paraded around the village. Martin carried a banner designed by Vicky which read:

Love Peace Justice.

We distributed some JfB leaflets and then sat around the main stage and listened to the Bands. It reminded me of the pop festivals of the early 1970s as the sun shone down on the Tolpuddle fields. Many people carried anti Bush Blair and Iraq War banners saying BLiar Out. Later, when Martin and Vicky had departed on their coach back to West Sussex I visited the Martyr's Museum which gives a good account of the birth of the English trade unions. I bought a Martyr's T-Shirt and a badge and then I drove back to Dorchester.

Next day I drove up to London. It was a brilliant sunny day as I drove along parts of England I had not seen before. I entered London via the M25, straight into a traffic jam. I stayed in London for two nights, but I felt a little ill from the moment I arrived. Maybe it was from the smog, or perhaps it was the comedown from the freedom of Tolpuddle.

While in London I responded by e-mail to News of the World reporter Danielle Gusmaroldi who claimed she wanted to support Barry. She wanted to visit him but I advised her that he would probably not agree to that. I went home on Wednesday 21.

On August 1 Margaret told me that the reporter had written to Barry, and he was mad at me as a result. If I done nothing he would be mad at me, and if I did something he would also be mad with me. Sometimes one just can't win.

I went to see him on Saturday 7 and we had a blazing row in which I threatened to walk away and pull the plug on the campaign and website. The row was quickly over and we had our tea and settled down for what turned out to be quite a good visit. I could appreciate how he felt about reporters, and I agreed with him when he said he didn't want visits from them. After all they had portrayed him as some kind of a monster, and helped the Crown's case against him, so how could he appreciate that we would now need to use them to try and turn around public opinion?

It was very hot in London and on the last night I had my head almost hanging out of Margaret's upstairs window trying to get some relief. I read later that the temperature was still 30° at 02.00.

When I got home I ended up with a very painful foot which my doctor said was a touch of gout probably sparked off by dehydration. Rich living the lads at work said, but if it was just a touch of gout I would hate to get the real thing as the pain was crippling. Unfortunately Shannon still demanded her walk through the fields and so I had to hobble like a cripple occasionally yelping with pain much to Shannon's amusement.

Conway Hall

2004-'05

On August 26 a new website www.barrygeorge.com replaced the original one which had run into a few problems.

On September 5 I read an e-mail from Scott Lomax telling me about a BBC reporter, Raphael Rowe, who hoped to make a programme about Barry. I made some discreet enquiries and I was told that 'He is a good guy, genuine'. I was happy with that recommendation and decided to contact him.

I phoned him the next day and we had a good long chat. He was quite up to speed having looked at the websites and appeal court links. I agreed to contact Barry and his solicitor to see if they might cooperate with a TV programme.

I later spoke to Pat Reynolds who was very enthusiastic when I mentioned Panorama, saying that Panorama could be seen as a turning point, the beginning of the end.

I next visited Barry on Friday October 8. I was suffering from a heavy cold, and family tensions were again running high, otherwise the visit went ok. On the way back to East Acton I saw on the headlines that the hostage Ken Bigley had been killed in Iraq. I got fish and chips and had quiet a miserable evening. 'Why the hell am I doing this?' I wondered, not for the first time.

The next day I went to a National Miscarriage of Justice meeting at Conway Hall in Red Lion Square. When I arrived there were a number of people waiting outside. I was a little early and waited some distance from them. A good looking young woman approached me and struck up a conversation. She quickly guessed that I was connected to Barry, which made me suspect that she was a reporter. She told me that her husband was in prison for murder but that he was innocent. To make it better she said that he allegedly had eaten the body of the victim. I didn't quite know what to make of her.

I met Hazel from MOJO and we chatted awhile. The Hall opened and we went in. I got a cup of tea and then I met Raphael Rowe. Scott Lomax texted me to say that he had arrived. He brought along copies of his book on Barry. Then Martin Jeremiah and Vicky arrived, shortly followed by Pat Reynolds. The meeting went well. It was interesting to meet Scott and Raphael and I hoped meeting Raphael would help to maintain his interest in the case.

On November 8 I watched a disturbing report on ITV News which said that there was a breakthrough in the Rachel Nickell case due to advances in DNA testing. Apparently the man now believed to be the killer was a serving prisoner. So it wasn't Colin Stag then. Could they mean Barry? He had been questioned about that murder, and some writers would sometimes try to link him to it. When I got the Daily Mail I saw that it was a deranged double murderer who had killed a woman and her child who was Rachel's probable killer. I was relieved that Barry was now effectively totally ruled out of that and the media could not make snide references about him in that context again.

On December 2 David Bieber was convicted of murdering PC Ian Broadhurst and wounding PC Roper. The court was told that he could have escaped without killing, but chose to delay so as to kill the already seriously injured policeman. He was given a whole life sentence.

On December 11 I made my seventh trip to London in 2004. While on the Tube to East Acton a dental plate fell out of my front tooth, which was embarrassing the next day as I opened my mouth wide for the prison officer to inspect. The prison visit went ok, and Margaret was in fairly good form.

That evening I met David James Smith at Starbucks in Hammersmith, where we discussed aspects of Jill Dando's murder which concerned me. David believed that I was on the wrong track but I was convinced that more people could have known of Jill's intention to visit her house on the day of her murder than we were led to believe. I also wondered how many people might have had keys to her house.

In early January 2005 there was a story in a Sunday paper about Sir Cliff Richard's religious views where he said that God would have to forgive Jill Dando's killer. I wondered if Sir Cliff was referring to Barry. Cliff, who was one of my childhood favourite singers, had been routinely interviewed by the police in an effort to find clues which might help to solve the case.

I drove to London on Monday 31. I had hoped to visit Barry on Tuesday and Margaret had promised that she would book it in good time. But she waited until Monday before phoning to book the visit. She then discovered that there were no visits allowed on Tuesdays. I was going to a public meeting in the House of Commons on Wednesday and so I had to wait until Thursday to visit him which lost me another precious day's holiday.

It was a short visit as his solicitor was also due to visit. Barry was somewhat stressed out as a result. He was concerned again that some of us would speak to the press. He got agitated when I told him that Raphael Rowe was interested in the Cutting Edge video, which I had in fact already loaned to Raphael along with a video of the trial reconstruction. He threatened to sue anybody who might use the Cutting Edge video. He then gave out to me for sending the cheque, saying that it had caused him stress. I was quite annoyed at his attitude. He then apologised for having a go at us, and asked if we could visit for his birthday. Sometimes he seemed as if he were still a kid, a large one.

In March I again made the trip to the London Saint Patrick's Day Festival. This time it was in Leicester Square in a gloomy location. It was a very cold day which matched my mood. I was not feeling very well. The day before we had tried to visit Barry, but when we got to Peterborough we discovered that there was no train connection to March. The bus would not get us there on time so it was a wasted trip.

Pat Reynolds could not make it due to a heavy cold. Andy Parr and Mick Gilgunn were there, and we collected some signatures for Christy McGrath and Barry's petitions.

I e-mailed Raphael Rowe asking about news on a documentary. He replied that Barry and his solicitor had made demands that Raphael could not comply with. Supporting Barry was often a struggle against the odds, as he seemed to see problems with everything we did or tried to do for him. I felt that a good opportunity was in danger of being lost and I decided to keep in touch with Raphael in the hope of some development.

On Sunday 27 there was an interesting report in the Mail on Sunday. Jeffrey Archer was hoping to appeal his conviction for perjury and was making a submission to the CCRC. Lady Archer's ex personal assistant Jane Williams had made allegations to the police before the trials of Archer and Barry, which both ran at the same time in 2001. The allegation was that Archer had hired a hit-man to kill his secretary Angela Peppiatt. Peppiatt had agreed to forge a 1986 diary which aided Archer at his successful 1987 libel action against the Daily Star, which had reported that he spent a night with prostitute

Monica Coughlin and that an envelope of money was passed to her by or on behalf of Archer. He was awarded £500,000 in damages.

Peppiatt bore a resemblance to Jill Dando and drove a similar BMW car. She also lived in the Fulham area. Her evidence at Archer's 2001 perjury trial helped to convict him and he was sentenced to four years in prison. Coincidently in April 2001 Monica Coughlin had a road traffic accident and died.

So, the allegation went, Jill was shot in a case of mistaken identity. The allegations were dismissed by Lady Archer. She was quoted as saying:

'I have long known false allegations were made to the police to assist the prosecution and undermine Jeffrey's defence. I am astonished that the police did not make known to us, as the law requires they should have done the preposterous claim that Jeffrey commissioned the murder of Angela Peppiatt.'

I would agree with Lady Archer but I wondered what the jury in Barry's trial would have made of this if they had been told. To me it was a clear example of lack of disclosure in both Archer's and Barry's trials.

I did not get to visit Barry for his birthday on April 15, but Margaret went along with a friend. I sent him a card along with a postal order, and Scott Lomax also sent him a card with the names of some well wishers on it.

In mid April I started work on updating the website and I added some interesting links to it. On Tuesday 26 Susan May was released after serving twelve years for the murder of her aunt. Susan had always protested her innocence and it was interesting that she was still officially 'In Denial' when she was released. We later exchanged a number of e-mails.

In late April JfB got an angry e-mail from the man known as Mr V. Scott Lomax featured V or Mr Vorms in his book 'The Case of Barry George', and on his website. It appeared that Scott may have sent Vorms something which he thought had come indirectly from me. I replied that JfB had not sent him anything either directly or indirectly. I and Michelle had discussed the article on Vorms and we both agreed that we would not want any other innocent person to be locked up.

I wrote to the CCRC suggesting that Barry's trial might have had a different outcome if the Archer allegations had been disclosed at the time of the trial. Somehow the Daily Mirror and Guardian got to know about my letter, (I didn't tell them) and they published a couple of articles. But that had the positive effect of letting the authorities know that we were watching everything. I did not believe that Archer would have hired a hit-man and my submission was merely intended to help Barry. I had read Archer's book FF8282 A Prison Diary and I was quite impressed at the fair unbiased way in which he had written about Barry.

May 25 was the fifth anniversary of Barry's arrest. Scott Lomax had tried to get an article published, and a regional newspaper had reported that he believed that Jill Dando had been shot by mistake. I forwarded Scott's article to a couple of papers, and I also sent a letter of mine to a few. The Limerick Leader's Barry Duggan phoned me and suggested that they would like to run a story based on my letter. I agreed and to help things along I allowed the photo of Barry which had been taken in prison to be used, with his mother and me blanked out. To my surprise the story dominated the front page of the county edition, under the headline 'Barry Did Not Kill Dando'. The photo accompanied the 'exclusive' article which was quite a scoop for Barry Duggan.

That evening he phoned to say that the Daily Mirror wanted to use the photo in a story, and wondered if I would sell it to them. I would not risk being accused of 'cashing in' and so while I agreed to them using the photo no money was exchanged.

The proverbial hit the fan on Friday 28 as the Mirror, Irish Independent, Star and Sun ran the story that I believed Barry was innocent, but of course it was the photo which made the story. I could not fail to miss how RTE ignored the story in their reporting of the regional weekly papers leading stories though they would often cover that paper.

Unfortunately in their report the Mirror incorrectly stated that I had taken the photo in prison, which would have been a serious breach of prison rules with negative implications for Barry. But otherwise I thought it was brilliant publicity for the cause. Unfortunately though the publicity was welcome I felt I had no choice but to make a complaint to the Press Complaints Commission about the Daily

Mirror, as I believed that Barry could be in hot water with the prison due to the inaccurate reporting.

I also realised that he would be hopping mad, and wondered if I would be allowed to visit him again. Michelle sent me a text message saying that she hadn't seen the paper and that I should have warned her. Others broke off contact with me for a few months but I was happy that the message had gone out loud and clear that we still supported Barry and that the battle would go on. I could live with the unpopularity it brought.

7-7

2005

On Sunday May 29 I phoned Margaret. After some small talk I asked her how Barry was. 'Fine, he phoned earlier'. 'Has he any news' I probed? Eventually she said that he had seen the Mirror report. She said that he was upset by it, but that a 'Screw' was standing by him so he could not say much. I then told her what the papers had said and she agreed it was good that it was reported that we still believed he was innocent. I asked if I was still welcome to visit him and she said yes, he would soon be sending out a visiting order. 'Oh God', I thought; 'now I will have to face the music'. I booked some holidays and my ticket planning to visit him on Sunday June 12. But then Margaret phoned and told me that my name was not on the VO. 'Fine' I thought, 'if he don't want me to visit that's ok by me'. She then mentioned how the Mirror had said that I had taken the photo of him in the prison. I explained to her about my complaint to his solicitor and to the Press Complaints Commission.

Later on the PCC published the Mirror's apology on their website. I was happy to let the matter rest there. I wrote a three line letter to Barry saying I would end the campaign and close the website if he didn't want me to visit anymore. The JfB campaign could not be run without the blessing of the prisoner. The timing was bad as Scott Lomax had only recently agreed to be part of the campaign, but the ball was in Barry's court.

Michelle phoned me on Sunday 5. She was pleased with the article but said I should have warned her in advance. She thought that Barry would be annoyed at the use of his photo, how right she was. As regards being in the doghouse, she said she knew what that felt like. She agreed that it was important that the message was out that we still supported him; otherwise people would think that we no longer cared.

In the evening Margaret phoned me. She had been to see Barry and again she had made the journey alone without any bother. She said that the whole visit had been taken up with him giving out about the article, even though she had nothing to do with it. She also said that he told her that I was not barred and that my name was omitted from the VO by mistake. He said that the prison officers had told him that I would have been allowed in if I had gone, but I knew that was not true. Nobody is allowed in without a VO. I told Margaret that I would visit him in July.

On Saturday July 2 I visited him for what I later believed was the last time. I told Margaret that I would not stand for any big arguments and would leave if there were any. He was immediately hostile towards me. I saw red when he accused me of being a coward who used moral blackmail against him by threatening to stop the campaign and website. He was very angry over the three line letter which I had sent him. He remained hostile so I got up saying 'I'm off, goodbye'. Unfortunately when I got to the door I couldn't get out as I left my pass with Margaret and had to ask her to bring it. While I was waiting Margaret engaged in an intense conversation with him. 'If he leaves now he'll never come back' she said. She then called to me to come back to the table, and Barry beckoned at me to return. I relented, apologised to the friendly female prison officer and went back. Barry then apologised for ranting at me and we had some tea. The rest of the visit passed without incident but I was struck by how angry he could be. At one stage a couple of officers in dark blue uniforms entered the visiting hall and Barry said that they were the heavy mob, to deal with any aggro. He then said that he could not discuss certain matters with me as he feared that I might run to the press. I did not argue but then he said that if I did anything to damage his case he would be very angry and the anger he displayed this day would be nothing compared with what he could be like. It seemed like he was threatening me. When Margaret spoke about my three dogs he joked that I had three dogs in case he came calling.

On Sunday afternoon I walked down from Holborn Station to the Covent Garden Transport Museum. It was quite interesting, with trolley buses, trams and trains. I saw how the tunnels were dug back in the 1800s. I looked into a war time train and was struck by how very gloomy it looked, like something out of the TV series Goodnight Sweetheart. On the walls were notices about what to do in the event of an air raid, and safety tips for coping with the blackout. I later walked around Covent Garden, over the cobbled roadway and then on to the Aldwych for a cup of tea and a sandwich. I also took a walk to the Appeal Court so as to remain familiar with the area in case we might be back there some day.

On Monday morning I left for home. It was announced over the tube-train public address that due to an incident there were disruptions on the Bakerloo line and Oxford Circus Station was closed. As I needed to change there for Euston I had to quickly work out an alternative route and time was tight. Fortunately for me Oxford Circus Station had reopened by the time my train got there and the rest of my journey passed without incident.

Three days later I was on standby at work when another driver mentioned a bombing in London. I went to the TV room and switched to Sky News where I saw that the terrorists had finally hit as had been feared ever since 9-11. Suicide bombers had targeted three underground stations including Kings Cross, the station we used when going to visit Barry. A bus had also been bombed and over the next few days the full horror was revealed. Over fifty people had died in what would become known as 7-7.

On Monday 11 I was on a late shift. Another driver handed me the Daily Mirror where I saw the report on the Jeffrey Archer allegations in relation to Barry, Jill Dando and the CCRC. The Media Guardian reported on the Mirror story and a London media website also featured it.

The following day it was reported that four young British Muslim's had been identified as the London bombers who died in the explosions. It was also reported that Sion Jenkins would face a third trial for the murder of his foster daughter Billy Jo Jenkins.

A week later I was contacted by a freelance reporter, Lynne Kelleher, who was in contact with the Daily Mail's Tom Rawstorne. I phoned Tom and he said that he had been asked to write an article about the evidence in Barry's case. He had already submitted it on the Friday that we spoke, but he was unsure if it would be published due to pressure of space due to the London bombing. On Tuesday 19 I met Lynne in a county town. We spent tree hours discussing the evidence and I gave her a CD of some work I had done. The next morning poor Jill Dando's face was once again on the front page of the Daily Mail. Tom Rawstorne's article was inside and it went into quite a bit of detail exploring the weaknesses of the case.

On Thursday the bombers again hit London, though fortunately the bombs failed to explode. On Friday it was reported that an Asian man had failed to stop when ordered to by police at Stockwell Station and was shot five times in the head. 'Brilliant' we all thought, 'they got one'. It was reported that the man who was wearing a bulky coat despite the heat failed to stop when challenged and vaulted over the ticket barrier, ran down the escalator and dived into a crowded tube train. The police caught and shot him before he could detonate his bomb. When the real truth emerged it was somewhat different.

It appears that he was wearing a light denim jacket, had used his Oyster card to access the station, and walked normally to the train where he sat down. It was a policeman who vaulted the barrier, ran down the escalator and dived into the train. The unfortunate man who was shot was the innocent young Brazilian worker Jean Charles de Menzes.

On Sunday 24 Lynne Kelleher's article was published in the Sunday World and the Irish Sunday People. It was quite good and questioned the forensic and identification evidence. I later got an e-mail from Scott Lomax which included a report on a speech by Michael Mansfield in which he said that he believed that Jill's killer was still at large.

When I next phoned Margaret she told me that Barry's father had finally visited him.

In early August the husband of Gracia Morton was found guilty of her manslaughter despite no body being found. Hamish Campbell had investigated her disappearance. Gracia had vanished after visiting her estranged husband Michael Morton at his Holland Park house in 1997. He was eventually charged when police found CCTV footage showing him visiting Gracia's flat the day after she vanished despite him claiming not to know where the flat was. A simple detail is often crucial in solving a case.

On Thursday 11 it was reported that Jean Charles de Menzes was identified as a suicide bomber suspect by a policeman who was relieving himself at the time. Jean Charles bore a resemblance but was a different colour to the suspect who lived in the same area and had similar eyes. It appeared that he was shot dead on that basis, i.e. due to mistaken identification. I drew comparisons with the fleeting identification by Susan Mayes of Barry and I contacted the press. Barry Duggan of the Limerick Leader responded and said he would run a story.

In late August I was given a copy of the October 1999 issue of Master Detective. In a six page report on the hunt for Jill's killer it was reported that in June '99 a Serb was arrested as he was about to leave the country. Apparently he resembled the suspect's e-fit, but the Dando police did not investigate him saying the 'Serb connection' was not a line of inquiry they were pursuing. It was also reported that in August '99 the police believed that they knew the identity of the man who organised the killing.

In an e-mail David James Smith seemed surprised when I said that the police had discounted the Serb line of inquiry at such an early stage. I decided to write to the CCRC about the Master Detective article. I sent them a copy explaining that I had already written to Barry's solicitor, and that I was reluctant to delay their investigation further. Then I got the idea that I should make a complaint to the Independent Police Complaints Commission. We had never complained to the police despite us being unhappy with their conduct. We did not see the point of complaining to the same police that charged him. It was the complaint by the de Menzes family that gave me the idea as until then I had never heard of the IPCC.

I ran up the complaint and submitted it on September 26 with a copy to Barry's solicitor. In an e-mail David James Smith dismissed the story about the Serb arrest and said that the e-fit was of the wrong man.

On October 1 Andy Gardner phoned me to say that the Sunday Mirror would be doing an article on Mr Vorms as they had interviewed him. I bought the paper and the story made interesting reading. Vorms claimed that he lied about where he was when Jill Dando was shot, his alibi being that he was working in a school at the time. He also said that he had done work on Jill's garden and that he hated her. It was revealed that he was an ex soldier and had once been suspected of reactivating deactivated firearms. He claimed that a policeman and policewoman had visited him asking why he had changed his alibi, and as to what questions the original Dando police had asked him. This all sounded very strange though he denied killing Jill. He also said that he did not believe that Barry had done it. He thought that the killer would have known that Jill would be at her house on that day. I thought that he was probably correct in thinking that.

On Thursday October 13 the Limerick Leader ran a front page story about the IPCC complaint. The Metropolitan Police wrote to me saying that they intended applying to the IPCC for a dispensation so as not to investigate it.

Margaret again visited Barry in late October and he was again complaining about the press. He said that he didn't care if we took off the website, and that his solicitor had said that the IPCC complaint would not help his appeal. I told Margaret that I could drop the complaint but she thought that it would not be a good idea. Michelle shared the same opinion, as did Scott Lomax. But the campaign had now run into difficulty as it appeared that it no longer enjoyed the blessing of Barry.

I contacted his solicitor and Scot informing them that as I no longer enjoyed the approval of Barry the campaign would begin to wind down. I also asked Scott to remove references to a campaign. However I decided that I would see the IPCC complaint through, as whatever the real truth was I felt that the police had not acted properly in the Dando investigation and we had to try and expose that.

I wrote to some politicians seeking their support for the inquiry and Willie O Dea, Jeremy Corbyn and Dave Horan responded. I also contacted the CCRC and the IPCC to inform them of each others involvement in the case.

On December 14 I got a message from Pat Reynolds. His son Kevin had been held by police for 36 hours in connection with the murder of the young model Sally Ann Bowman in Croydon. Twenty police officers had searched Pat's house. Kevin was released without charge when DNA was checked. Kevin complained that he was the only one arrested despite BBC Crimewatch identifying thirty people in addition to fifty initially named by members of the public. Pat felt that only for the DNA evidence it could quite easily have been another Barry George type case. Mark Dixie was eventually convicted of the murder. But it seemed strange that as the police

Mike Burke

had Dixie's DNA from the word go why did they feel the need to ransack Pat's house? Could it have been as a result of his campaigning activities I wondered?

In late December the IPCC asked me if I would agree to a CCRC request for a copy of my complaint. I was then informed that the police request for a dispensation was rejected and so the investigation would go ahead in due course. It was a little victory but coupled with all the recent press reports there could now be no doubt that we were going to fight back hard.

Margaret visited Barry on December 22. When I told her of the IPCC decision to investigate she complained that Barry would be upset as the people in the prison would be getting on to him about it. I replied that if we were to take too much notice of that we might just as well give up and accept his conviction.

Panorama

2006

Early in the New Year I received a couple of e-mails inquiring about the campaign rather than about Barry which was unusual. Then Scott Lomax told me there had been a Sunday Express article which had quoted me. We contacted the reporter Camilla Tomlinson who sent us a copy. It was quite a good article which revealed that I was no longer welcome to visit Barry, and that Margaret was now his only regular visitor.

On January 21 I phoned Margaret. I asked her if Barry still put Michelle's name on visiting orders. To my surprise she replied that he always put our three names on them. I had understood that my name had been removed, so perhaps Camilla's article had influenced somebody.

I got a letter from Willie O Dea saying he had been in touch with the IPCC and that he was reasonably confident about the upcoming investigation.

In March Margaret told me that Jeremy Moore had requested that we would not issue any stories to the media in the run up to the CCRC decision. I passed that on to David James Smith and to my surprise he replied that Jeremy Moore had phoned him and there was a possibility that he could visit Barry, he was due to meet Jeremy on Friday 24 to discuss the matter.

On Saturday I received a text message telling me that Jeremy Moore had issued a press statement. It mentioned the two witnesses who apparently saw armed police at Barry's flat, and that medical evidence would show that Barry could not have committed the crime. The big news was the release of another hostage, Norman Kember, in Iraq.

The following Saturday the Irish Daily Mail ran a two page spread by Bob Woffinden in which he re-ran his Serb theory, that Jill Dando was executed as a result of the 1999 war in Kosovo.

I was again contacted at work by reporters on Monday April 3. One was a researcher seeking to contact Jeremy Moore and Michelle with a view to making a TV documentary and I forwarded their contact details. On Saturday I got a text telling me that Michelle would be on the TV 3 programme 'The Big Bite', along with John O Connor and Hazel Keirle. Michelle said that Barry had asked her to be his public 'Face'.

On April 13 I watched the programme. Michelle said she 'knew' that Barry was innocent; as she had asked him and he said he was. John O Connor, former head of the Flying Squad, explained why he thought it was a professional 'hit' probably done by a team. But he didn't try to explain why the 'hit' didn't take place in Chiswick where Jill lived or how the assassin could have known that she would be in Fulham on that day. But overall it was a good programme, positive.

A VO had arrived at Margaret's and so I would be again visiting London on Sunday 30. I had an unpleasant journey on Saturday. I was sat in the quiet coach in the company of two loud railway 'buffs' and a noisy toddler who insisted on running up and down the carriage, hurting himself in the process. After sharing my dinner of burger and chips with a friendly pigeon in Euston I walked down to Kings Cross Station to check out expected train cancellations for the next day. Kings Cross would be closed on Sunday so we would have to go from Finchley Park Station.

We were late getting to Peterborough so we had to take a taxi to the prison which cost us £35 including a small tip. On the way I read an article in the Sunday Express by James Murray. The headline read 'FAMILY FEAR FOR DANDO's KILLER'. It had a large photo of Jill Dando and inserts of Barry and Susan. It was another Michelle / MOJO story claiming that Barry was not getting the correct medication for his epilepsy. Margaret refused to look at the article.

Barry was in good form though a little anxious as we were late, being almost the last visitors to arrive. He was unshaven, though I noticed that he had shoelaces. He said he agreed with the Express article provided it had been first approved by his solicitor. Margaret then told him that it was what he wanted and he said if it went through his solicitor it was ok, but if it didn't there would be trouble. He then reminded me how angry he could be if things were done without his approval, referring to the awful argument we had back in July. I was annoyed but I said nothing. I was a little concerned that he was again trying to threaten me. That type of behaviour undermined my belief in him. He then spoke about the late David Dobbins and Eugene O Mahoney and the replica gun which they had taken from his flat. He claimed that the 'gun' had been intact when it was taken and so he thought the damage which resulted in the exposed spring had happened after it left his possession. He also denied that it was him in the photo of the man in the gas mask posing in the SAS style photo. I reminded him that the police said he took the photo and he said 'how could I do that?' I mentioned self timers and he said that his camera did not have one.

He complained that for the second time a prison officer had removed his copy of the book ALL ABOUT JILL.

He then spoke about the book Bent Coppers, which had a reference to Detective John Gallagher. He also said he would like to have a visit from David James Smith, Scott Lomax or Andy Parr, but Scott and Andy were never approved by the Home Office.

When the visit ended Margaret and I walked around March, looking at the church near the station.

The Wishing Well in East Acton seemed to have died since my last visit there in December. There were hardly any customers and sport blared from TV sets all around. Wayne Rooney was in the news as it was feared his broken toe would prevent him from playing in the World Cup. And somewhere in London a fire bomber was on the loose.

I returned home on May 1 finishing Razor Smith's book A Few Kind Words and a Loaded Gun along the way. Razor has been in and out of prison for much of his life. He had met Barry at Belmarsh and John McVicar published an interesting account of the meeting. Razor's book had quite a depressing end with him being sent down for life. Shortly after I returned home my computer again crashed and I had to get a new Hard Drive.

Diary extract July 8 2006. *I recently had to have the hard drive replaced on my computer which cost me 205 Euro. David James Smith is due to visit Barry early this month if all goes well. Raphael Rowe is in America researching for a BBC documentary on Barry. He is consulting experts with regard to the single particle. He phoned me up last week seeking Michelle's details which he had mislaid. I had a letter published by the Irish Daily Mail two weeks ago marking the fifth anniversary of what we believe to be the wrongful conviction of Barry, and I also e-mailed letters to other papers and had a pop at RTE's Joe Duffy. Not a lot happening, Damilola Taylor case is still in the news.*

On July 20 Andy Gardner phoned me. He told me he was now a freelance reporter. Later Margaret phoned to say that the VO had arrived.

The next day I got a call from a Mail on Sunday reporter, Mr Rice who asked if he came to Ireland would I speak to him. I agreed and he said he would be over the next day. I then became a little concerned as I was due to visit Barry and wondered if speaking to the reporter would cause another row. Fortunately he had also called to Michelle which I thought might take the flak off me.

The report appeared on Sunday and referred to the Panorama programme which was being made by Raphael Rowe. It mentioned two jurors who were having doubts and who apparently were willing to appear on the programme. It also mentioned that FBI agents criticised the Met Polices handling of the single particle evidence.

On Monday Raphael asked me not to discuss the programme with MOJO. I replied that I had fallen out with them in 2001 due to the News of the World article. But I feared that a last minute hitch might have negative consequences and so I texted Michelle asking her to urge discretion on MOJO. She replied that they hadn't known about the programme.

On Thursday August 31 I again went to London. It was a good trip, uneventful except for a poor man who finally cracked after over three hours in the 'quiet' coach listening to a hyperactive loud child.

On Friday I went to Mario's café for breakfast. Later Raphael Rowe phoned Margaret and I spoke to him.

At 16.45 I met Andy and Chris Parr outside East Acton Station and we had a cup of tea in the Sunrise café. We discussed Barry and the background to the Jill Dando murder. Chris was interested in making a television dramatisation on the subject.

The following day Margaret and I visited Barry. He was OK which came as quite a relief to me as I feared he would be doing his nut with me over press reports.

Sunday was a bore and I spent a lot of it walking around East Acton and Shepherds Bush. I photographed the memorial at Wormwood Scrubs to the three policemen who were murdered there in August 1966. Michelle, Susan and Barry were walking there on the day and Michelle saw the shot men lying on the ground and quickly got her brother and sister away. She later told her mother how she saw the men lying there.

When I returned home I sent some photos of Barry and family to Raphael Rowe for use in his documentary.

In mid-August following a BBC Radio 4 programme I contacted Professor Elizabeth Loftus PHD. Elizabeth is an American memory expert based in Stanford University. Elizabeth later expressed concerns over eyewitness testimony which largely helped to convict Barry. She agreed to be added to the list of 'concerned', her concern being based on witness identification.

Her website reads: 'Elizabeth Loftus studies human memory. Her experiments show how memories can be changed by things we are told. Facts, ideas, suggestions and other post-event information can modify our memories. The legal field, so reliant on memories has been a significant application of the memory research'.

Unknown to us on September 4 a Forensic Science Service report prepared for the CCRC dismissed the FDR evidence which dammed Barry as inconclusive. In their opinion it provided no support for the prosecutions case that Barry had killed Jill Dando. It would be another year before we became aware of that.

Raphael Rowe phoned me to say that the Panorama-George programme would be broadcast on September 5. I took a day's holiday to watch it because as luck would have it I was on a late shift and I feared I would not get to see it. At 07.33 Pat Reynolds sent me a text message to say that BBC Radio 4 News was reporting on the programme every half hour. It was also on BBC News 24, and RTE Radio 2FM. For me at least it was exciting news as this was the biggest development since the 2002 appeal and I felt I had helped in some small way to make it happen.

The Telegraph reported that the programme cost £250,000 to produce and took Raphael two years to investigate. In response to criticism of Raphael a spokesman for the BBC said: 'Raphael is a first class investigative journalist with five years experience reporting from a range of BBC outlets . . . He is a wholly appropriate presenter for this programme, which meets the usual criteria for impartiality, fairness and accuracy'.

At 21.00 I settled down to watch Panorama. It began with Raphael saying to Barry over Margaret's telephone 'so you didn't kill Jill?' . . .

'course not, replied a surprised Barry. Then the photo of Barry which I got taken at Whitemoor was shown alongside the prison envelope in which it was returned to me after the prison refused to allow Barry to have it. CCTV footage of Jill Dando on her last journey and a clip of 29 Gowan Avenue was shown, and Helen Doble's 999 phone call was played. It ran through Barry being questioned, his visit to HAFAD and Susan Bicknell's meeting with him. It was Susan's first day at HAFAD and she recorded the time of his visit. Two days later Barry called back asking staff to recall the exact time of his earlier visit. A week later Susan typed an account of her meeting with Barry for the police and she wrote the time of his visit as 11.50. That seriously undermined the Crown's case that Barry shot Jill Dando after 11.30, returned home by a circuitous route to change his clothes and then went to HAFAD. There would not be enough time to do that and be at HAFAD before 12.10 according to Raphael who walked the Crown's suggested route. But Susan revealed that at court she was unwell and suffered a breakdown shortly afterwards. She felt upset that her illness might have caused the jury to doubt her and that they might have convicted Barry as an indirect result of her illness.

Barry's fear of being questioned about Jill Dando's murder due to his being questioned in 1992 over the murder of Rachel Nickell was covered and video footage of his live I.D. parade was shown. Richard Hughes took an interest in number one but nobody picked Barry. Then Susan Mayes was shown picking out number two, Barry, on October 5-2000.

It was then revealed that witness Charlotte de Rosnay had an affair with a policeman on the case, DC Bartlett. Charlotte failed to pick

Barry but in the taxi home Susan Mayes revealed how she had picked Barry. Charlotte later said she might have picked Barry but for his beard. Barry's solicitor Jeremy Moore described Charlotte's affair with DC Bartlett as inappropriate.

Regarding the Kensington Pistol Club which Barry tried to join in 1982, it was pointed out that Barry would not have been allowed to handle a gun as he could not supply the required references.

Then it was revealed that the FBI had stopped testing for firearms discharge residue due to the risk of contamination. A pistol was fired and it was demonstrated how residue got on the clothes of the woman who fired the shot. The residue showed up as white specks on a detector, like dandruff on a dark jacket at a disco. The woman then walked around Raphael Rowe without touching him, and the detector then showed residue on his clothes. A Massachusetts lawyer then explained how false positive results can occur. At Barry's trial the forensic scientist Robin Keeley had said that innocent contamination was unlikely.

The Reverent John Hale did not go on air but it was pointed out that he claimed to have seen armed police going into Barry's flat. Charlotte de Rosnay was said to have claimed off camera that DC Bartlett told her that the police had concerns about how they handled Barry's coat. Keeley did not know that the police had sent the coat to the photographic studio where it might have become contaminated until ten months later.

Professor Marco Morin, an Italian forensic expert cast doubts on whether the particle was even gunpowder, and claimed it could have come from other sources. Forensic science is not always reliable, he said. The single particle was not enough to link Barry with Jill Dando and should not have been used at the trial.

Raphael then spoke to jury member Jane Herbert. Jane was worried about being interviewed but said that she didn't think that the evidence was enough to convict Barry. On the evening of the conviction she phoned the Old Bailey at 22.55 and left a message on the answer-phone. She claimed that she felt very angry, outraged, tricked after leaving the court. Janet felt alone, isolated, at the hotel where they stayed, and it appeared as if the case was being discussed among groups of jurors, which would have been a breach of the judge's directions. An anonymous male juror confirmed that discussions did take place outside the jury room, but he described them as chit-chat, not deliberations. Janet said that she knew that due to hearing remarks over breakfast. Raphael then described how the jury was divided for four days, and wondered if hotel chats over the weekend influenced them.

Jeremy Moore then said that questions ought to asked about the weekend discussions and that the CCRC would be asked to do a full investigation into the juror's deliberations. Raphael said that new evidence would be sent to the CCRC. The police declined to be interviewed by Panorama.

The programme drew to a close with Barry saying over the phone 'I haven't committed this crime, right? don't deserve to be here'.

Other prisoners could be heard in the background. Raphael: 'so you didn't kill Jill Dando?' Barry: 'of course not'.

The programme ended with my photo of Barry in prison.

It was interesting to hear the opinions of the Italian forensic scientist, Professor Morin and the American experts and lawyers, but I felt that there was nothing that we didn't already know. However I totally failed to anticipate the effect the programme would have on the general public.

Later down at the pub some people were really excited by it, it was a real eye opener to them. When I got home and turned on the websites guest book I got a taste of the public reaction, and it was stunning. Normally the 'site was rarely responded to but suddenly there was a great interest, and the reactions were mostly of the opinion that Barry's conviction was shaky to say the least.

Unfortunately there was a little ill feeling among some that they did not get any credit. I would not be drawn into that argument and remained focused on the bigger picture.

On Thursday the Guardian reported that Hamish Campbell felt that the CCRC was treating him like a liar in relation to the 'unarmed police' claim.

On Friday the Irish Star reported that Willie O Dea called for a re-trial at least, and he said he was impressed by my efforts. Michelle was not over impressed with the article as it referred in the headline to

'Dando's Killer'. She forgot to tell me that on the same day she had recorded an interview for RTE's Marian Finucane Saturday morning show.

I recorded the programme. It was in my opinion a tough interview. Michelle referred to the Panorama programme as 'viewer friendly'. She claimed Barry would be incapable of murdering Jill Dando due to his medical conditions and Marian pointed out that epilepsy would not rule one out as a killer.

On Thursday 14 on advice from the Mayor of London's office I wrote to the Metropolitan Police asking if Operation Oxborough had traced, investigated and eliminated a certain individual. I was interested whether or not they would answer. Margaret visited Barry on the same day. Two weeks later I again went to London and Margaret and I visited him. He was upbeat about his prospects and believed he would soon be freed. He then asked me to give him details of the IPCC complaint as he was wondering if I had done his case some damage. He said that the website was inaccurate though he could not give me one example. I told him that if he wanted I would withdraw the complaint and remove the website but he said that would be selfish of me. I felt a bit like Bart Simpson, damned if I did and damned if I didn't.

The following day I returned home. It was a nightmare journey. I left Margaret's at 07.30. East Acton had no underground service so I had to dash to the bus stop and take a bus to Shepherds Bush. I then took the Metropolitan line train to Paddington where I changed to the Bakerloo line for Harrow Wealdstone. Unfortunately services ended at Queens Park as an earlier lightening strike damaged signals and I had to wait over a half hour for another train. I had to rudely force my way into the train when it arrived as it was jam packed. It was utter chaos at Harrow Wealdstone, and nobody seemed to know where the trains were going. I boarded a Liverpool bound train only to be later told that it was Manchester bound. I decided to stay on it until Watford Junction and wait there for the Liverpool one. I had to wait there for another hour.

Luckily Margaret had given me a couple of chocolate bars and these kept me going until I arrived at Crewe where I was able to get tea and sandwiches. I was wrecked when I arrived home and I was in pretty foul humour for a couple of days.

David James Smith later told me that he would be visiting Barry on October 4.

The IPCC also confirmed that the complaint was on hold until the CCRC would report.

David did visit Barry. He was striving for that visit since March. He thought that the interview went well. Not as good as he hoped but not as bad as he feared. He was struck by Barry's slow careful way of speaking.

He asked if there were any unused photos of Barry and I suggested that Margaret might let him use a nice one of her and Barry from his teenage years. She agreed it could be used and I also e-mailed some photos which I had, hoping to portray Barry as normal rather than some kind of a monster. As David was not a supporter but in fact believed that Hamish Campbell got it right I was looking forward to the article. I was just hoping that it would be carried in the Irish version of the Sunday Times.

I made another request to the police under the freedom of information act asking if Detective John Gallagher was the same detective who was mentioned in the Graham McLagan book Bent Coppers. What sparked my interest was that as part of an investigation into corrupt police a Detective Gallagher had (quite correctly I understand) removed information from a file and substituted it with an altered replacement.

Andy Parr phoned me on Thursday 26 to tell me that the Sunday Times would be running a story. He also suggested that we might meet Fine Gael's chairman Tom Hayes TD in the New Year. (We never did)

Margaret visited Barry on Friday and he had a plaster on his hand which prevented him from opening the wrapper on his cheese biscuits. He felt that the prison officers did not take his injury seriously and he said that he did not get an x ray or any painkillers. During the week I had begun reading another book The Rachel Files written by Detective Inspector Keith Pedder, about the Rachel Nickel murder investigation. It was a terrible crime but what made it more interesting was that at the time of it being written the real killer was not identified, even though he was actually locked up in a mental hospital since 1993 when he again stabbed a young mother to death and also suffocated her daughter.

On Friday I asked my local shop to keep me a copy of the Sunday Times. I read the article with interest. I couldn't understand the front cover of the magazine until I held it away from my eyes and realised that it read KILL JILL. Apparently that was a play on a film titled KILL BILL. The article was pretty fair to all concerned. I was interested to see that the Home Office had tried to stop David visiting. He was told unofficially that the Home Secretary John Reid did not want the interview to go ahead as if it did it would not look very tough on crime. The Sunday Times threatened legal action and the Home Office backed down.

Barry revealed that he used to have ambitions to return to work with the BBC. David saw Barry's new submission to the CCRC which was put together by his solicitor Jeremy Moore and barrister Jeffrey Samuels along with Edward Fitzgerald QC. Barry's original defence team were criticised by the new lawyers for not letting Barry give evidence. 'The jury especially in a serious case, likes to see and hear from an accused. The jury might well have considered it highly unlikely he was capable of having committed this crime but may instead have concluded that police, under pressure, were driven to arrest the "local weirdo." (In Barry's 2008 retrial he again did not give evidence) Samuels seemed to be very critical but I believe Mansfield did his best at the time having regard to Barry's sensitivities about his mental health and desire to keep his previous convictions out of the case.

The article ran through Barry's stalking and photographing of women, his use of different names and pretence of being Freddie Mercury's cousin. David revealed that one or two of Jill Dando's previous boyfriends were not best pleased that she was about to marry somebody else. He mentioned 'another man' who became a suspect when police realised that he had lied about having been just a platonic friend of Jill's.

The article finished with descriptions of two strange men. The first was an account of a meeting in a south London pub with Mr Vorms who claimed he drove Alexander Baron to Jill's house. Baron was allegedly blackmailing her over some pornographic photographs involving her. (Smith points out that they were nonexistent) Vorms waited in the car while Baron went to collect the £40,000 blackmail money, and he claimed that Baron shot her when she refused to pay. The car then wouldn't start and Vorms ran away. He claimed to be the sweating man at the bus stop. Vorms was reported to police early on, and Smith suspects that he made the report himself.

Mr Baron confessed in 2005 to Hamish Campbell that he was the real killer. Baron lived not far from Vorms. Baron walked out when Campbell pressed him to give an account of the killing. Baron has a criminal record for a stalking related offence from 1997 when he threatened to 'slit the throat' of a DSS female benefits officer. The article ended with the assertion: So it wasn't Vorms; it wasn't Baron. It ended with the question if it wasn't Barry George, then who was it who killed Jill Dando?

I take issue with one point in the article, the alleged absence of any plausible alternative explanation or the emergence of anything new that pointed elsewhere, away from Barry. There *is* something new, whether it means much is debatable but it has been brought to the attention of the police who have examined it.

I phoned Margaret in the evening asking if she had seen it but she hadn't. Scott Lomax was also tied up and hadn't seen it either. When David sent me a link I forwarded it to Scott suggesting we link it to the website. Michelle said the article was good but inaccurate. She did not elaborate.

Later we added the link to the website, but the article was soon taken off line. It appears that there was a threat of legal action as the article was quite critical of Barry's original defence team.

On Monday 30 I received a reply from the police telling me that Detective Sergeant John Gallagher from the book Bent Coppers and Detective Constable John Gallagher who investigated Barry were not identical. I think they meant there were two detectives called John Gallagher. I had not noticed the different ranks. Barry's solicitor wanted to know where I got my information regarding the Gallagher's and so I forwarded on the FOIA reply.

In a separate reply to my September 14 question the police revealed that they had spoken to the person I referred to in my question who had given them background details and details of movements on the day of Jill's death. They also revealed that the person was not a suspect in the investigation of 'Miss Jill Dando'. I considered that remiss of the police.

Margaret and I visited Barry on Monday December 11, his seventh Christmas behind bars. I was surprised when he announced that he was going to sack his solicitor Jeremy Moore. I advised him not to as the CCRC was due to report at any time. He said that he was 'pissed' with the CCRC, insisting that he would be freed as there was no evidence to hold him. I explained that it did not matter how many people might believe that he was innocent, the CCRC was the only way to go, and only the appeal court could either free him or order a retrial. But my advice seemed to fall on deaf ears. I did send him a postcard from Holyhead asking him if it was not too late to reconsider his actions. I also sent him a small postal order.

When I got home I e-mailed his solicitor accordingly. Jeremy Moore visited him on Thursday and believed that he had calmed down again.

And so another Christmas came around. The Limerick Leader ran an article on my visit to Barry and my hopes of him being cleared. Privately I was losing hope that his case would be sent back to the court of appeal as I felt that there was probably political pressure being exerted to prevent that. Many prisoners including Jeremy Bamber had recently been given whole life tariffs and so I was not over optimistic.

At the end of the year there was a glimmer ahead but no shining light.

Breakthrough

2007

In mid January we again feared that Barry was going to sack his legal team but again he calmed down. I was a bit put out at hearing from his mother that he blamed us for his continued imprisonment, after all if he had heeded our advice back in 2000 he might never have been tried much less convicted. I wrote to him to that effect.

Meanwhile the big news of the day was Channel 4s Big Brother and the row between the Indian actress Shilpa Shetty and Jade Goody.

February came and still no news. After four years the campaign seemed to be fizzling out. Pat Reynolds and Andy Parr had more or less dropped out probably as a result of the ending of their campaign for Christy McGrath. Christy had decided to finish serving his sentence in Ireland which effectively ended his campaign to be cleared of murder. Personally I agreed with his decision to return home.

I met Michelle briefly on Sunday 5. I asked if she had any plans to visit Barry but she hadn't at that time. She was a little unhappy with Jeremy Moore for reportedly speaking to the News of the World without consulting her or MOJO.

Margaret phoned me in the evening. I asked her about the solicitor and she said she thought Barry wanted two of them. 'Strange', I wondered, 'why two, what game is he playing'? She then said that in a phone call a week earlier Barry had spoke about the possibility of being transferred to a Yorkshire prison. That would make visiting him very difficult for her and would probably involve an overnight trip.

Later I e-mailed Scott Lomax, Margaret Renn and David James Smith. Scott replied that if Barry were transferred then he could easily visit him if he should ever be approved. David James Smith thought Barry would be crazy to sack Jeremy Moore in the run up to a CCRC decision saying that the submission to the CCRC was as good as he could get and wondered why they would want to move him at all. On Monday I e-mailed Jeremy to try and find out what was happening, and I filled him in a little on MOJO. I had been planning to visit Barry again at Easter but thought I might now go earlier though really I had little influence on him.

Jeremy replied saying that he was still on the case though he knew Barry had been in touch with another solicitor. He said that he was merely interested in getting the case back to appeal and winning that and he was not interested in other agendas. He asked me to stay on board until the hoped for appeal.

Later in the week I read the amazing story of a female NASA astronaut who drove 1000 miles to Orlando airport to confront a love rival. She was reported to be dressed in a big coat wearing a wig and diaper and armed with an air gun and other kidnapping implements. Fortunately the other woman got away. It made me think of Jeffrey Upfill Brown's evidence when he described Jill Dando's fleeing killer as appearing to be wearing a wig. Can we be sure he saw a man?

I phoned Andy Parr. He said that his brother Chris was still interested in making a TV drama on Barry but that the TV companies said that the case was not a sympathetic one. Speaking to Margaret on Saturday 18 I said that I probably would not be over for the London Saint Patrick's day parade due to the ending of the Christy McGrath campaign. 'I suppose you won't be over anymore so' she said. It did appear as if the campaign was fizzling out but I thought I would at least try and keep it going until his hoped for appeal hearing, and then review the situation.

On Sunday 25 I worked on a letter seeking support for the IPCC investigation. I e-mailed a copy to the leader of the Conservative Party David Cameron. His private secretary Laurence Mann replied in quite a positive way saying that David would keep a close eye on events.

On Wednesday I got an e-mail from John O saying that there were 236 prisoners convicted between 1999 and 2003 still awaiting the setting of their minimum tariff. Barry would be one of them.

One evening while walking with my dogs I got a text message from Pat Reynolds saying that an 'Ann Summers' gunpoint rapist had been convicted. The man had committed the rape in 1996, threatening to blow the brains out of the victim and then casually walking away, but he had evaded detection until advances in DNA made it possible to charge him. He seemed to have a fascination with TV presenters. However since 1996 he had been convicted of other rapes and I was told that he was in custody at the time of Jill Dando's murder. So that would have ruled him out of the frame. I was puzzled at a reference he made about BBC TV newsreader Emily Maitlis who he described as his 'special lady'. The witness Alison Hoad had described a man who sounded like Barry say that a 'special lady' lived in the general direction of where Jill Dando lived. That was used as evidence that Barry knew where Jill lived.

On Good Friday in Limerick city I had to tell a young teenager off for interfering with my vehicle. He walked away but then returned and loitered close by. I noticed that he had an object in his hand concealed by the side of his right leg as he stood behind a rubbish bin. I realised that it was a gun, a dirty black looking object. A woman who I was speaking to was stood between him and me. I immediately phoned the Guards and realising that I was speaking to them he walked away. He then adopted the role of an innocent child playing with a toy. However the woman who was watching closely told me that it was just a pellet gun, but it would give a nasty sting, or maybe knock an eye out. Meanwhile in Dublin the Guards wondered if a man who was shot dead on his doorstep was killed as a result of a parking dispute. Those incidents make me wonder if Jill Dando's killing could have been as a result of a senseless trivial matter which escalated out of all proportion.

Margaret again told me that Barry was concerned in case of media reports in the run up to a possible appeal. I e-mailed MOJO's John McManus asking that they would respect his wishes. John replied that he would respect the request and said that he would pass it on to Hazel Keirle.

I also got an interesting e-mail about 'Zip' guns. I had never heard of such things but I saw that one could download details of how to make one from the internet. They basically consist of a pipe with a crude firing pin and would be very inaccurate so requiring a very close shot to be effective. In Jill Dando's case no aim was required but I believe some of those guns are fired by back pressure from a hard contact. That might explain the gun muzzle bruising to her head.

In May the IPCC were also in touch saying that they had been in touch with the CCRC and that they could not say how long more the ongoing CCRC investigation would take. They were considering getting on with investigating my complaint and sought my opinion. I replied that I would be in favour provided that Barry's solicitor had no objections.

On May 25 I again went to London. On Saturday I went to the post office for a postal order for Barry. I then had a nice cup of tea in what was Mario's café, now under new ownership. I glanced over the Irish general election results in the Irish Independent and then met Margaret on her way to the station. Being a Bank Holiday weekend the trains were packed though we did manage to find a couple of spare seats.

Barry was in quite good form. He took me to task over the reply which I had received under freedom of information regarding the identity of the Detective John Gallagher. Barry was still not convinced that the Detective Gallagher involved in his case was a different person. I was also a little puzzled due to the wording of the reply which said they were not identical.

The IPCC were again in touch and said they would decide in Mid June whether to commence the investigation.

Andy Parr phoned and said that a TV dramatisation of the Jill Dando / Barry George story was again on the cards and that his brother Chris was anxious to again meet with me. I said that I would pop over soon but I thought that Barry would reject the idea out of hand. Andy said that the programme could go ahead in any case.

At long last we got some good news which cheered all our spirits. I had planned to visit London on Saturday 23 June to meet with Andy, Chris and Don Shaw, scriptwriter. However on Wednesday the CCRC gave their long awaited decision which was that the case should go back to appeal. That was based on the importance which was given at the trial to the single particle of firearms discharge residue. I decided to bring my trip forward and go on Thursday as Margaret was already going to visit on Friday. Good timing, I thought.

On Thursday I got the 06.55 train. I was due to take the 11.10 Stena Ferry but unfortunately a body was found on the rail line near Dublin and so all services were delayed causing me to miss the boat. Instead I took the 14.15 Irish Ferries and eventually I arrived in East Acton just in time for a pint before closing time. I then went around to Margaret's. She asked me if I had told Ann Moneypenny of MOJO that we were visiting Barry. I was surprised as I thought Ann had long departed the scene. Of course I hadn't told her but Margaret said that Moneypenny had phoned and was speaking for an hour. Meanwhile back home Tom was also phoned by Moneypenny looking for news.

Margaret and I went to visit Barry the following morning. On the way Raphael Rowe texted me wondering if Barry would give him the first interview *when* he was released. I thought Raphael was over confident but of course he didn't personally know Barry. Barry was in good form, joking with us. The visiting hall was unusually quiet with just a few visitors. We had the usual tea and biscuits and then I asked him if he was happy with his defence team. He said he was and that his barrister would be Fitzgerald. Edward Fitzgerald QC I presumed. He hoped that he would get bail. He said he would reserve his decision regarding his first interview. At least he was honest enough to say that, I thought, no false promises. We also discussed clothes for his appeal. The visit soon became very intense and I was pleased to get out of there. The prison officers were amused by his exaggerated embrace of his mother and we had to drag ourselves away. Those visits could be exhausting at times.

On Sunday about 09.00 I was upstairs shaving when the phone rang. Margaret shouted up that Barry wanted to speak to me. He was absolutely furious as he had just seen a Sunday Express front page headline about him. Michelle had given the Express an interview but he assumed that I was the culprit. He threatened anyone who had anything to do with it with an injunction. We had quite a row then as I yelled back at him that neither I nor Margaret was involved with the Sunday Express story.

On Monday afternoon I wrote a sharp letter to him but softened it with the postal order. I then met Andy and Chris Parr, along with Don Shaw at East Acton's Sunrise café. We discussed Barry and I was impressed by Don's knowledge of him. They had made a TV drama some years earlier called BAD COMPANY about the Bridgewater Four. Margaret Renn had highly praised that programme and had told me that her partner Jim Nichol was the solicitor who eventually got the three surviving convicts cleared. The journalist the late Paul Foot had campaigned tirelessly for them. I told them that I had informed Barry and his solicitor that something was afoot and they said they would contact both Barry and the solicitor.

When we finished we all walked over to Fitzneal Street so they could see Margaret's house. As soon as they left I went in where Raphael Rowe was waiting. He said there would probably be a Panorama programme update in the next week or two. He thought that Barry would probably not face a retrial. I asked him about a possible police backlash and he seemed to think it had already begun in the utterances of Nick Ross who had asked if Barry had not done it who then had? I said if Nick kept asking maybe we could give him a reply. Raphael replied that it was possible to make a TV programme along those lines but it was not his job. I then said that if Barry was freed I would consider asking the police to reopen the case.

When I got home I had the usual huge welcome from my three dogs. Tom told me that MOJO's Moneypenny had been on the phone looking for me also. One of the lads at work joked about the tea and biscuits which he read about in Lynne Kelleher's report on how we had celebrated Barry's good news.

The big news now was Tony Blair's departure from 10 Downing Street. Then on Friday the terrorists resurfaced in the UK with a car bomb in London and on Saturday a car bomb in Scotland. It was an unpleasant welcome for new Prime Minister Gordon Brown.

I e-mailed Barry's solicitor telling him a little of the TV drama plans. He replied that he had no problem with it.

I was a little surprised to see on the news that a number of trainee doctors were arrested in connection with the London and Scotland bombings. I guess being a doctor does not preclude one from trying to commit murder.

Margaret told me that Barry was talking of getting bail. He had mentioned that on our last visit. I told the solicitor that though we were not wealthy we would do our best for him if bail was set. He replied that bail was unlikely and that the appeal might be in October or November.

On October 19 Raphael Rowe phoned to tell me that there was an advertisement in the Stage Magazine about the Chris Parr / Don Shaw drama. Raphael cautioned about such a project saying that there were dangers, especially as Barry had an appeal in the pipeline. But I think I had done everything above board, by running the idea past Margaret, Barry and his solicitor. The programme had the working title 'Celebrity'. Don said he wanted to do the production because he believed that Barry was innocent.

Meanwhile Nick Ross was continuing his assertion that Barry was guilty and I felt that we should respond. I contacted the police with another probing Freedom of Information request but due to legal reasons I can not elaborate on that.

On Sunday I was browsing the internet as Don Shaw had mentioned something about the Sunday Times. What came up was a report by James Murray in the Sunday Express about 'Celebrity'. The report incorrectly claimed that Raphael Rowe and the BBC were involved, and included negative stuff about Raphael's past. The BBC also got a knock due to recent bad publicity surrounding phone in competitions.

While I was reading Raphael phoned wondering who had spoken to the 'Express'. Michelle was quoted and was reported as reacting negatively. As always in such matters the truth is elusive, but the end result in my opinion was the death of an excellent opportunity to show the world that Barry was innocent.

On Thursday the Irish Daily Mail published a letter from me in relation to Nick Ross. I was informed that Barry's appeal would be heard on November 5, 6 and 7. *Fireworks night* . . . David James Smith said. Perhaps there would be fireworks, I mused.

On Friday a report from the Lancet claimed a link between cannabis use and psychosis. I am no medical expert but I had often wondered if there might have been a link between Jill Dando's killer and psychosis. I am aware that some around her would indulge. I still wonder if Jill knew her killer, who somehow knew she would be at her house on that day.

The Sunday World carried Lynne Kelleher's article about Celebrity. That raised the interest of the Limerick Leader who thought I was involved in the programme. I explained that my involvement was probably over, and that I had merely helped Don and Chris with background research, which was more or less the case.

Margaret and I visited Barry again on Saturday August 18. Kristin, a producer from the Panorama team drove us. We were in March in time for a nice cup of tea in Johanna's café. Barry seemed well and I tried to convince him to give Raphael Rowe an interview but without much success. He told us he was having a bail hearing on Wednesday and warned us not to reveal that to the press. At one stage Margaret asked him 'who do you think you are, Mansfield?' as he made his arguments as to why he would have to be released.

On Wednesday 22 Barry was refused bail.

Second appeal

2007

Barry caused us all a minor panic in early October by publicly sacking his legal team. The Mirrors Susie Boniface phoned asking what was happening but it was total confusion. Panorama's Kristen confirmed it. Raphael Rowe then phoned me and explained that Barry was unhappy as his new QC would not be available for the first day of the appeal. But fortunately Jeremy Moore remained on the case and William Clegg QC joined the team.

On Thursday 18 Michelle texted to say that Barry was back in Belmarsh. In reply to my question of September 14 the Met police advised me that if I thought I had new information on a case which was officially solved then I should contact the investigating officer. I immediately began working on material which I would later send to Hamish Campbell. I was reluctant to do so but it was a matter which I felt I could not ignore.

As I travelled to London on November 3 I read an open letter from Nick Ross to the Appeal Court telling them why he believed that Barry was guilty. On Sunday evening I watched the Cutting Edge update on Channel 4 before having a quick pint in Chiswick's Tabard pub.

On Monday I entered the Court of Appeal via the back door. Raphael Rowe was present along with Kristen, Bob Woffinden, Scott Lomax, David Perrin and David James Smith. Margaret Renn was also present but we didn't meet. There was some delay as the prison officials wanted Barry to appear in the Belmarsh green and yellow boiler suit. In 2005 the Mail on Sunday's Peter Hitchens described such attire as a 'clown suit' when the hapless Michael Stone was forced to wear one for his appeal into his dubious conviction for the murder of Lin and Megan Russell. Eventually common sense prevailed and Barry entered wearing his suit and looking fairly clean shaven. Doctor Susan Young sat with him throughout the appeal and the Daily Mail later made sneering remarks about the 'blonde' Dr Young.

Here I have again in the interests of accuracy used quotes and paraphrasing from the 2007 Appeal Courts Approved Judgement. The actual quotes will be prefaced by the numbers which appear on the approved judgement.

The appeal was heard by the Lord Chief Justice Lord Phillips, with Lord Justice Leveson and Mr Justice Simon.

William Clegg QC and with Mr Jeffrey Samuels for the appellant.

Orlando Pownall QC and Jonathan Laidlaw QC for the Respondent.

The LCJ was critical of a letter which was sent to them (Nick Ross) and of two TV programmes (Panorama and Cutting Edge) and said the court would come back to that later. Shortly after proceedings began there was a dramatic outburst from a Mr Paul Cleeland, an ex prisoner who alleged that Mr Clegg was not doing his job properly. The LCJ politely asked him if he would let the court deal with it 'in our own way' and Cleeland was escorted from the court quickly pursued by Duncan Campbell of the Guardian.

Mr Clegg informed the court that a second particle of FDR was found on the outside back of Barry's Cecil Gee coat after the trial which could only have got there due to contamination. He said that he wanted a retrial with a jury fully informed about the particle evidence.

The new evidence on which the appeal was based was outlined. Dr Ian Evett worked for the Forensic Science Service (FSS) from 1996 to 2002. His role there included assisting scientists to present evidence in court in a clear logical way.

In conversation with a colleague during Barry's trial Dr Evett discussed the FDR evidence. He was led to understand that the effect of the evidence was 'neutral', that it lent no positive support to the claim that Barry had fired the gun which killed Jill Dando. But the newspaper reports at the time suggested that undue weight was being put on the evidence, causing him 'vague unease'. He discussed this with his line manager who suggested that he discuss it with Mr Keeley.

16. Dr Evett and Mr Keeley met on 19 November 2001. At that time Dr Evett was in the course of developing with colleagues, who did not include Mr Keeley, a technique called Case Assessment and Interpretation (CAI). The object of this is to clarify *before* evidence is examined and analysed the likelihood of the examination achieving particular results on two different hypotheses or propositions. This technique facilitates the drawing of appropriate conclusions from the results actually obtained on the examination.

17. At his invitation and with his assistance Mr Keeley applied the technique to the likelihood of different findings that he might have made on, as we understand it, carrying out the examination of the pocket of the appellants coat that he in fact conducted. His conclusions related to two different propositions (1) that the appellant was the man who shot Jill Dando; (2) that the appellant was not the man who shot Jill Dando. Mr Keeley estimated that the likelihood of his finding no FDR particle had been 99 in 100 on either proposition, and the likelihood one of a few particles as 1 in 100 on either proposition, and the likelihood of finding lots of particles as 1 in 10,000.

(These figures being intended simply to signify 'remote in the extreme') on either proposition.

18. The significance of this was that, in Mr Keeley's opinion the finding that he in fact made of a single particle had been 'neutral'. It was no more likely to have come from the gun that killed Miss Dando than from some extraneous source. Mr Keeley confirmed to Dr Evett that he did indeed consider the discovery of a single particle had been neutral.

19. Dr Evett considered the judges summing up in the light of his discussion with Mr Keeley. He recorded his views in a note. Those views were that the summing up was unbalanced in the way that it presented the FDR evidence to the jury in that, while it paid much attention to the fact that it was unlikely that the single particle would have come from an extraneous source, it paid little attention to the fact that it was equally unlikely that the particle would have come from the gun that killed Gill (Jill) Dando.

Dr Evett took no action in relation to his conclusions. He later explained that his overall view was that, although the presentation of the FDR evidence was protracted and confusing, he felt that the jury should have gained the right impression-assisted in no small measure by the evidence of John Lloyd.

The CCRC requested the FSS reappraise the FDR evidence which was given at the trial. In their report dated 4 September 2006 the authors Dr Moynehan and Miss Shaw summarised their conclusions at the outset of their report:

The FDR evidence is thus inconclusive. In our opinion it provides no assistance to anyone asked to judge which proposition is true.

This precisely echoes the views expressed by Dr Evett and Mr Keeley'.

End quote.

Mr Clegg called witnesses from the FSS, Doctors Moynehan and Evett. Dr Moynehan stated that the particle was neutral and confirmed the views of the 2006 FSS report. He said that under new FSS guidelines a single particle would be considered to be of no evidential value. Dr Evett then confirmed the note of his conversation with Mr Keeley.

Pownall called Mr Keeley. He confirmed the accuracy of Evett's account of their discussion. He said that at the time of the discussion it was his view that FDR evidence was 'neutral' and it still was. His evidence had been given before the new FSS guidelines and had they been in place then he would have added a rider that the particle provided no information as to whether the wearer of the coat committed the offence. He said that he had intended to convey to the jury that it was no more likely that the single particle came from a gun fired at the time of the murder than that it came from some other source. With hindsight he agreed that he should have made that clearer in his evidence.

The court resumed on Tuesday at 14.00. I was puzzled when Pownall referred to a size nine footprint from a popular trainer type shoe which was found in the bloodstains at the crime scene. I do not know if the size is the actual size of the unidentified footprint. Barry is closer to size eleven, my size.

Pownall seemed to be labouring as he made his closing speech and eventually the LCJ wound it up by saying it was four thirty, court would resume on Wednesday. Pownall came back stronger on Wednesday. He said that the case against Barry was not based solely on the particle. He referred to Susan Coombe and the silver gun in the shoebox from 1985, 'that gun has never been traced'. He mentioned Alison Hoad and the 'special lady' comment which Barry allegedly made. There was also the identification evidence and the single polyester fibre. It was a compelling circumstantial case and the FDR particle lent it powerful support.

Clegg gave an excellent closing speech. He asked if the jury was misled by the particle evidence. It was most critical to the case and time was wasted on it, but it focused the jury on the wrong question. Nobody understood the neutrality of the particle or that it was possible that it came from an innocent source. It should have been a submission rather than taking up a whole week of the trial.

There was some discussion about Keeley's evidence and it was agreed that he was not asked the correct question in relation to the particle. Rather than focusing on innocent contamination a question should have been asked as to the likelihood that it came from the gun which killed Jill Dando. One of the judges then asked who should have asked that question and it was decided that the prosecution should have. Referring to Mr Justice Gage's summing up Clegg said Gage had told the jury that the particle formed an important part of the case. Without it the case would be weaker.

48. The judge introduced the conflict of evidence between Mr Keeley and Dr Lloyd as follows:

"If you are sure that it is in fact firearms discharge residue, are you sure that the particle was not deposited on the coat as a result of what we have all been calling innocent or adventitious contamination?

Mr Keeley's evidence is of very considerable importance when you are considering both these questions-as indeed, let me make it clear, is Dr Lloyds evidence of very considerable importance.' He went on to add that tests carried out under the supervision of Mr Keeley showed that FDR would more often be found on an individual firing a gun than not.

End quote.

There was some amusement as Clegg struggled with the word adventitious incorrectly saying 'advantageous', and Leveson said it for him. 'Without the particle you must be very cautious of finding guilt,' Clegg continued. 'Mr Justice Gage never described the particle as neutral. Keeley's caution in giving his evidence was not picked up by the judge or jury. They were both misled by the Crown. The fresh evidence renders the case unsafe'. He went on to say that there was no ID to confirm that Barry was the killer. The two men who saw the killer did not identify him. Mr Hughes described seeing a dark wax jacket, not the coat containing the particle. Susan Mayes saw a man standing by an untraced car four hours earlier. Mayes and Barry both lived locally. Her evidence was not strong. The polyester fibre was extremely common. Barry's coat would shed many fibres but none were found on the victim. The route to the conviction was illegitimate.

Pownall was then asked if the Crown would seek a retrial if the appeal was successful and he said yes. The LCJ then said that judgement would be reserved but he didn't expect that they would take long.

Outside the courtroom I met Susie Boniface from the Sunday Mirror and she, Scott Lomax and I went to the cafeteria for a chat. While there Dr Susan Young came over. I asked her how Barry was and she said that she had to persuade him not to intervene during that morning's session. I knew that he would have liked to say something in his defence but was glad that she had calmed him.

Later I met Hazel Keirle and her daughter Tanya in the George pub. Hazel said that I should try to attend for the appeal findings and I said I would if possible. Scott was doing an interview for BBC Radio Sheffield and I escorted him to Bush House. I then made my way to East Acton and had a pint, then went to Margaret's and had a nice dinner. I went home on Thursday feeling that it had been an inconclusive week. The big news that week was of another awful murder in Italy, that of British student Meredith Kercher.

I was back in London on the following Thursday for the appeal findings, using up the holidays which I had hoped to keep for Christmas. I again entered the court by the back door and had tea in the cafeteria where I met James Cohen. We took our seats in the courtroom and I was shocked to hear an announcement 'appeal dismissed'. I and I think everybody else thought it was all over. I was absolutely stunned and then somebody said that the announcement was in relation to some other issue. What a relief.

Unlike the 2002 appeal copies of the findings were not handed out in advance. Just a short reading was given with the full findings to follow. The appeal was allowed at 10.15 and the conviction was quashed with a retrial ordered. It took a while before it sunk in that Barry was no longer a convicted murderer.

The Approved Judgement explained that the Court of Appeal was asked to determine if the conclusions which could be drawn by the jury from the FDR evidence were correctly given.

Pownall had described the FDR to the jury as 'compelling evidence of his (Barry's) guilt'. Keeley was asked if it was significant that only one particle was found rather than 100 or 150? Answer No.

Keeley elaborated to the appeal court in a manner that might have been helpful to the jury. He dismissed the possibility of secondary contamination as 'most unlikely'. The appeal court had some difficulty reconciling some of Keeley's evidence at the trial with the evidence he gave before the appeal court. The manner in which he had given his evidence was likely to have given the jury the impression that because innocent contamination was 'most unlikely' the particle must have come from the gun which killed Jill Dando. The appeal court judge believed that Keeley's evidence left both counsel and the trial judge with the same impression.

In Gage's summing up he understood based on Renshaw and Keeley's evidence that the particle provided cogent support for the other evidence, and it formed an important part of the prosecution case. Gage said that the prosecutions case would be much weaker if the FDR evidence failed to stand up. In that case the jury would have to be very careful before concluding that Barry George was the murderer. He then went over the conflict in Mr Keeley and Dr Lloyds evidence. He described the evidence of both as of very considerable importance.

The appeal judges found that Mr Justice Gage correctly directed the jury based on the evidence of Renshaw and Keeley, which supported the prosecutions case that Barry fired the gun which killed Jill Dando. Gage did not consider that their evidence was 'neutral'. In reality their evidence gave the impression that innocent contamination was unlikely, that the single particle came from the gun which killed Jill Dando.

'In that respect their evidence at the trial was in marked conflict with the evidence that they have given to this court with the result that the jury did not have the benefit of a direction that the possibility that the FDR had come from the gun that killed Miss Dando was equally as remote as all other possibilities and thus, on its own, entirely inconclusive. In the light of the way in which Mr Keeley now puts the matter, we have no doubt that the jury was misled upon this issue'.

The appeal judges acknowledged that there was circumstantial evidence capable of implicating Barry, and that Mr Clegg had accepted that by conceding to a retrial if the appeal was successful.

They concluded by saying that it was impossible to know what weight, if any, the jury attached to the FDR evidence. It was equally impossible to know what verdict they would have reached if they had been told by the Crown scientists that it was just as likely that the FDR came from some extraneous source as it was that it had come from a gun fired by Barry.

'The verdict is unsafe. The conviction will be quashed'.

The appeal findings changed my mind on an important matter. I had always suspected that Barry's coat had been taken to the photographic studio so as to create an innocent explanation for the finding of the FDR if it became necessary. I had up to then believed that the FDR was from the gun which killed Jill Dando and as I believed that Barry was probably innocent my reasoning for the finding of the FDR was that it was planted in his pocket. The new evidence removed that suspicion but opened another.

When the surviving six of the McGuire Seven had their convictions quashed by the Court of Appeal in 1991 the court had this to say about forensic scientists:

"We are of the opinion that a forensic scientist who is an adviser to the prosecution authority is under a duty to disclose material of which he knows and which may have some bearing on the offence charged and the surrounding circumstances of the case. The disclosure will be to the authority which retains him and which must in turn . . . disclose the information to the defence . . . We can see no cause to distinguish between members of the prosecuting authority and those advising it in the capacity of a forensic scientist. Such a distinction could involve difficult and contested enquiries as to where knowledge stopped but, most importantly, would be entirely counter to the desirability of ameliorating the disparity of scientific resources as between the Crown and Subject". 'However the court acquitted the scientists of any deliberate attempt to mislead the court at the original trial'.

<u>Forensics. Dr Zakaria Erzinclioglu.</u>

The same I am sure should have applied to Barry's case.

Outside the courtroom I was phoned by a Limerick Leader reporter and I simply said I was pleased. He asked if I would give Radio 95 FM an interview but I declined saying they could use the comment which I gave to the Leader.

I moved away from the crowd and went to the cafeteria for a cup of tea. I met Susan Young who said that Barry was very happy. I had a chat with David Perrin and James Cohen and then we went across to the George pub where I had more tea.

James asked me why I might think that Barry could be guilty and we discussed some possibilities, such as could he have committed the crime unconsciously, as say a sleepwalker or schizophrenic might. But we concluded that if that were so it was most unlikely that he would or could have covered up the evidence. David then interjected to say that the only reason why we might suspect him was because he was accused in the first place. If he had not been accused then we would have no reason to suspect him. Though such a discussion might be viewed as stupid seeing he just had his conviction overturned I think it was important that we did not blindly accept his innocence. I believe it pays to be open minded.

We met Ann Moneypenny and Tanya, along with Andy Gardner. Michelle later arrived and we all went upstairs for a meal.

I then went to East Acton. I looked up the website in an internet café and was impressed by all the e-mails and positive messages on the guest book. I went to see Margaret but was a little disappointed that she didn't share our joy. She had thought that we would be bringing Barry home and she was upset that he would have to remain locked up awaiting another trial. I was surprised later while visiting other relatives to see her on the ITN News at 6. She complained that he was still locked up asking 'why, why?' It was a brilliant piece of reporting, showing her as a genuine anguished mother rather than someone playing it up for the camera.

Meanwhile the Evening Standard focused on the anguish of the Dando family and Alan Farthing. He was said to be disappointed. I read through the papers next day as I made my way home. The Star asked 'Who else is in the frame?' They listed some possibilities: a criminal's revenge for Crimewatch, the Serbs, an ex lover, a stalker, or armed burglars. They claimed that a Scotland Yard 'source' had said at the time of the murder that a friend or person from her past might have killed her after an unknown personal row. I was quoted as saying 'I would like the police to solve the crime and get the real killer. I have always thought Barry was innocent. There is a good chance justice will now be done'.

Jill's brother Nigel Dando, according to The Star, issued a challenge to Barry, 'NOW PROVE YOU DIDN'T KILL MY JILL', and suggested that Barry might be given the chance to go in the witness box and give an account of his movements on the day Jill was killed.

I later read that at this time the defence team in preparation for the retrial requested FORENSIC ACCESS to review the forensic evidence, including the single particle. Roger Robson, one of the UK's most experienced textile fibre scientists led the work.

When I got home quite a few people expressed their agreement with the appeal result but I wondered how they would feel following the retrial when all the evidence of his previous convictions and transgressions would be aired in court. It was not a nice prospect.

On November 24 I e-mailed the Met Police requesting that certain matters be investigated. I also posted a hard copy to Hamish Campbell via registered mail.

It was reported that Robert Napper was charged with Rachel Nickell's murder. He had been arrested over a double murder of a mother and her daughter some time after Rachel's killing but he was unfit for trial and was sent to a mental hospital.

I was a little surprised not to get any answer from the police and so on Thursday December 13 I wrote about it to Willie O Dea TD. He replied that he would write to the Home Office. On Friday I heard on RTE Radio that Barry was back in the Old Bailey for a bail hearing. The big news now was the funeral of Meredith Kercher, and the Princess Diana inquest.

On Thursday 20 Sean Hoey who was accused of the Omagh bombing which killed 31 innocent people including two unborn was cleared after a 36 day non jury trial. The judge severely criticized the police handling of the investigation. Mr Hoey was represented by Orlando Pownall QC.

On Christmas Day Margaret told me in a phone conversation that Barry might be moved to Manchester Prison as his solicitor was finding it difficult to visit him. If he was moved she said that she would be unable to visit him as it was too long a journey for her.

Retrial

2008

I am standing in a general store. Coarse sacks of produce are stacked all around the floor. A horse drawn carriage draws up outside pulled by two white horses. Two men alight. They are dressed in old fashioned red tunics and plus fours. They have a grim looking strong man with them whose arms are tied. They bring him in and take him up a ladder to the loft and I realise that there is going to be a hanging. Not wishing to be present I go outside and find myself in a small poorly lit village or hamlet. I hear a crash from inside. A short time later the men bring out the body and put it on the carriage. They then drive to a nearby building.

I awoke and made my way to the Old Bailey.

In January 2008 Robert Napper pleaded not guilty by video link to the murder of Rachel Nickell. Margaret told me that Barry had been moved to Manchester. Michelle suggested that I might like to stay in the Mitre Hotel when visiting him. I planned to go over on February 15, stay overnight in Manchester, visit him and then go to London. I hoped that Margaret might meet me in Manchester but she would not travel alone.

I found Manchester a little confusing but the hotel was easy to find as it is right next to the Cathedral. It is an old hotel but clean cheap and cheerful. Next morning after a nice breakfast I made the short walk to HMP Manchester, formally known as Strangeways. I checked in at the visitors centre and then entered the main prison. I was frisked and checked with a metal detector. Then I was escorted through the grim prison to see Barry. There were high barbed wire fences all around, numerous locked doors, corridors and stairs. My escorting prison officer told me that everything had changed since the 1991 prison riots which had started there and spread like wildfire throughout the UK prisons.

The visiting hall was quiet with just one other visit in progress. There were more prison officers than visitors but they were quite polite. Barry was disappointed that there was no coke in the vending machines. He was in good form, cheerful and optimistic. He wore a dull blue jumper with a red bib which I presumed was to identify him as Cat A. It was interesting to be able to talk to him alone, the first time since his arrest. He said he would like some changes to the website, and a visit from David Perrin. He still felt angry towards Paddy Hill and Don Hale, nearly six years after their visit. He thought that Orlando Pownall would not be prosecuting at the retrial. We also spoke about the John McVicar book and I told him of McVicar's description of how he allegedly killed Jill Dando. The visit was cut short after barely one hour. We were told that he could apply for an extended visit if he knew in good time when visitors were coming. I texted some visiting information to Michelle as I made my way back to the hotel. I picked up my bag and then took a train to London.

In March I received a reply from the Met Police saying that they had investigated the matter which concerned me, and that a new statement was with the Crown Prosecution Service. I forwarded the information to Jeremy Moore.

I again visited Barry on Friday 28. He was ok and we had a 90 minute visit. He was very confident and felt that the Crown's case would collapse. I thought he was over confident. He thought it was all thanks to him that he would be cleared and I resisted reminding him that it was possibly thanks to him that he was accused in the first place. I later popped down to London and met some relatives. Margaret wasn't home so I got the train back to Holyhead and got the night boat home.

The Daily Mail reported on May 6 that Orlando Pownall was off the case. Jeremy Moore informed me that the retrial would commence on Tuesday June 3. I went over on Monday and checked into the Chiswick Court Hotel.

It was raining as I walked up Fleet Street on my way to the Old Bailey. I popped into Lets Eat for a cup of tea and a roll. When I came out my umbrella stuck and my hand slipped when forcing it open. Blood flew as my thumb was gashed by the broken wire frame. I walked up the street in pain holding my hand up in an effort to stem the bleeding. I managed to buy some plasters and wrapped it up though a stitch or two was probably required. I was lucky that my shirt wasn't spattered. I could just imagine a headline, 'Blood spattered uncle arrives for George trial'. I met Michelle in Nero's coffee shop in Newgate Street along with MOJO's John McManus who was there on other business. I cleaned myself up in the toilet, washing away the blood.

As we approached the court a few photos were taken but it was low key. We had to wait in reception until someone could escort us to Court No 1. Before 9-11 we could go up on our own but security had tightened since then. Some time later I had to go to reception to escort a stand in solicitor upstairs, and the next morning I had to wait for the same solicitor to come down to escort me up.

Upstairs we met Raphael Rowe who introduced us to a BBC reporter who would be covering the case. I became aware that Michelle was unhappy with Barry's legal team and I guessed that had something to do with MOJO. Duncan Campbell of the Guardian was also there as was John McVicar. Michelle later had a go at him over his book and to his surprise I sympathised with him over the drowning of his dog Clem. Later on I noticed Hamish Campbell looking at me. I had written a couple of letters to him but we never spoke.

Retrial

The trial judge was the Hon Justice Griffith Williams. Jonathan Laidlaw QC for the Crown. William Clegg QC along with Mr Jeffrey Samuels and solicitor Jeremy Moore for the defence.

There did not appear to be anyone from the Dando family present. Doctor Susan Young was allowed to sit with Barry unlike in 2001 when the prosecution objected to her presence in the dock. Barry looked scruffy as he was wearing an old blue sweatshirt, though Michelle said that he had got nice court clothes. Later in the week he was allowed to wear them.

Michelle and I were sat behind the lawyers, under the public gallery facing the jury benches, which I thought was a bit odd. When they came in I tried to avoid looking directly at them as I feared that we might be open to an accusation of intimidation or trying to influence them. (When I returned in July Michelle had moved to the other side of the courtroom, out of direct sight of the jury).

The main legal argument that week revolved around the admissibility of evidence. Laidlaw argued strongly that the FDR should be included, but eventually it was ruled out. Mr Clegg informed the court that recent surveys had shown that gunpowder traces can be found in 15% of underground trains and buses.

At the 2001 trial Michael Mansfield had claimed that by the end of the trial the particle would have disappeared altogether. I doubt if he could have imagined that it would take seven years but finally his words came to pass. But by 2008 the law had changed and damaging evidence inadmissible in 2001 would be used.

The trial would focus on bad character evidence. Barry's following or pestering women around the streets of Fulham and beyond, taking photos of them and frightening them. There was a long list of women who felt that he had harassed them and that was whittled down to what was considered to be acceptable examples of bad character. One example which caused some amusement and which was ruled out was an incident where he presented a woman with a bunch of flowers on Saint Valentines Day.

It was also claimed that he tried to create a false alibi at HAFAD. Witness identification would again be most important and again this would include evidence not allowed in 2001. E.g. the recollection of Richard Hughes that the man he claims to have seen resembled the comedian Bob Mills, who in some photos can resemble Barry.

Some of the CPS people seemed bored and I was amused to see one of their female staff doing a crossword. There was difficulty selecting a jury. The candidates were warned to expect the trial to last up to eight weeks. It was hoped to have a panel of 20 but out of 49 people called they ended up with 15. Eventually a jury of eight women and four men was selected.

Outside the courtroom I spoke with Mr Clegg and Samuels. We discussed Julia Moorhouse, the woman who described being spoken to by a man who could have been Barry approx an hour after Jill Dando's murder. I felt that her description of the man was too like

Barry to be coincidence, and as she reported the meeting to police straight away on that day it sounded genuine. We agreed that the man she met was probably Barry but disagreed as to whether they met before or after he had visited HAFAD. The Crown claimed it was before, which would support their case.

I met Scott Lomax on Friday and we had a chat and a quick drink. Michelle, Serj Sinclair and Tanya joined us. We had a friendly chat but Serj seemed to be a little sarcastic towards Scott's writings. I felt uncomfortable, embarrassed, and Scott seemed a little annoyed.

Next day Margaret Michelle and I visited Belmarsh. I decided to ask Barry about Julia Moorhouse but he replied 'no comment'. I assumed the role of interrogator.

'Now you are making me suspicious, did you see helicopters while speaking to the woman?'

He replied 'everybody in Fulham would have seen them'.

'Did you see them' I persisted.

'I just told you that I did'.

'Yes or no, answer the question'.

'Yes' he finally said.

'That is all I need', I ended.

That confirmed to me that he had met Julia in the street near HAFAD at about 12.30, she recalled the man speaking about the circling helicopters. But it was unclear if he was on his way to HAFAD, or had he already been there.

On Monday the jury came in and the prosecution began. It was interesting to hear Laidlaw say that only those closest to Jill Dando would have known that she would be visiting her Fulham house on the day of her death. That was a subtle but important difference from 2001 when it was incorrectly claimed that only her fiancé and her agent were aware or her plans.

Laidlaw told how Barry had a fascination with female TV presenters, had taken thousands of photographs of women in the street, and that he once recorded a route which a woman took so as to trace her to her home. He had an interest in guns and lied about his alibi. His various name changes were mentioned; his ownership of replica and blank firing guns, and the mock gun attack at the home of David Dobbins. The killing of Jill Dando was carried out by an individual, acting alone with no rational motive.

That evening the media were again having a field day, with the London Evening Standard headline claiming 'DANDO KILLER HID PHOTOS OF TOP TV WOMEN'. Barry did have photos taken from a television, but they were not hidden.

I went home on Tuesday. The evidence which followed for the rest of the week was bruising with evidence being given by various women who were followed by Barry, who sometimes turned up at their door saying 'now I know where you live'. It appeared that I was wrong in thinking that he had learned his lesson following his release from prison in 1984. Somebody asked on the websites guestbook 'is he being tried for murder or stalking?'

I went back to the court on July 8 for the last day of the prosecution evidence. A witness Clair Dawson gave an account of a number of encounters with a man she met at a Fulham bus stop in August 1998. The man wore a 'Queen Crew' jacket. She guessed that he was from a flat nearby where posters of Queen were displayed. He chatted to her and she became aware of his presence over the next few months. She worked in a wine bar, and one day the man entered her workplace. Clair hid from him. She complained to her boyfriend Greg who saw the man one day and he told him to leave her alone. The man denied pestering her but she was not bothered by him again. The implication of her evidence was that the man, who might have been Barry, backed off when confronted by a man.

Laidlaw tried to show a link between Jill Dando being a Baptist and Barry's interest in that church. I thought Laidlaw seemed rattled when Clegg accused him of scraping the bottom of a deep and empty barrel.

A document was read out concerning Jill's burglar alarm. It appears that cleaners would sometimes have difficulty setting it, and she would sometimes leave a note asking them to set it. I noted with interest that there was some difficulty setting it on Friday 23 April, three days before her murder. I understand that she and Alan Farthing visited the house on Saturday 24, and so it would appear that they were the last visitors prior to her death. Did they set the alarm correctly I wondered?

I was surprised to hear that Jill's clothes were given to a charity shop in the summer of '99 by Judith Dando and Jenny Hingham. Unfortunately the clothes were no longer available to test for evidence such as DNA. I consider that remiss of the police who should have preserved the house and its contents. The sale of the house could have been suspended pending further investigating.

Later in the cafeteria I met Martin Brunt of Sky News. I had been in touch with Martin via e-mail. We spoke about the case and Martin was hoping for an interview with one of us, preferably Michelle. I didn't think he had any hope there but I would have considered giving an interview if I thought it would be useful. I described some aspects of the murder which bothered me and Martin seemed to be interested. He said that thanks to improved record keeping since the 1987 sinking of the car ferry the Herald of Free Enterprise in Zeebrugge passenger movements can now be more accurately examined. As a consequence a willing police force should have little difficulty in establishing passenger movements. My interest in car ferries stems in part from a report that Jill's assassin entered the UK by ferry to avoid more stringent airport security checks. When I went to get the teas in I met David James Smith and he joined us. He knew Martin and they discussed ongoing developments in Portugal relating to Madeline McCann.

Defence

The court began late on Wednesday even though we were all in our seats at 10.30. I looked all around trying to form an impression. I counted 68 glass panels in the Grand Dome. The sword was on the wall behind the judge's chair, so he was the senior judge that day. Flat screen TVs were dotted around the courtroom. In front of me a female TV reporter was sleeping soundly. Then somebody told me that Barry was unhappy with me again, and that Private Eye had taken the mickey out of the prosecutions evidence.

Finally at 11.30 proceedings began. Mr Clegg made an application for 'No Case to Answer' but the application was rejected. The actual defence would start on Monday 21. First there would again be a trial within the trial to decide if no inference should be drawn from Barry exercising the right to silence. It was like a rerun of the 2001 trial, with even the possibility of a reduced jury due to holiday bookings.

The court ended early on Thursday and so I decided to take another walk around the Gowan Avenue area. It was a lovely sunny day as I walked the streets of Fulham. Copes Fishmongers, the last place Jill Dando visited was no longer there but I timed myself as I walked from Crookham Road where Barry used to live, back to 29 Gowan Avenue. I walk quite fast and it took me about five minutes. I observed how close the doors of the Gowan Avenue houses were to the footpaths, about two footsteps at most I estimated. I went home the next day.

On the following Thursday there was a small victory as the judge ruled that no inference should be drawn if Barry remained silent. Michelle texted to say that the single polyester fibre was now being treated as the big evidence, even though it was too small to be fully analysed. Roger Robson of FORENSIC ACCESS had earlier reviewed the fibre evidence. His two reports revealed that Jill's coat had been removed from her and left in the open air for up to nine hours while police, paramedics etc came and went. The original investigation had not eliminated the possibility of the fibre coming from anyone at the crime scene, Jill's other clothes or from the people who were close to her. Mr Robson was the first defence witness. He faced a rigorous cross-examination by Laidlaw for about half a day. He is reported to have given his findings in an objective and controlled manner.

On Monday 21 it was reported that former Bosnian Serb leader Doctor Radovan Karadzic was arrested in Serbia for war crimes committed in Bosnia.

I was quite annoyed when I read reports of Doctor Michael Kopelman's medical opinion on Barry. It seemed to me that Barry's inappropriate behaviour was being blamed on the overall family. I sent a protest to Jeremy Moore. In my opinion one is responsible for ones own actions and it is a cop out to try and blame ones bad behaviour on the family.

I e-mailed Martin Brunt one day asking if Sky News would investigate an aspect of the Dando case which puzzled me. He replied that interest in Barry's case appeared to be waning and he was now concentrating on the Madeline McCann story. I thanked Martin for his interest and said I would not be giving any interviews. I was disappointed and wondered what had happened to the old tradition of great investigative journalism? Nowadays only the 'official truth' seems to get reported.

Closing addresses.

I wasn't present for Laidlaw's closing address so I have based this section on a Guardian report of Thursday July 24. The evidence linking Barry George to the murder of Jill Dando could not be dismissed as unhappy coincidence he said. He admitted that the evidence was not straightforward but said that the prosecution 'did not lack any confidence' that George shot Jill. He said that there was no DNA evidence and 'no obvious candidate for this killing, nobody with anything approaching a rational motive to kill this woman'.

But he said things began to fall into place nearly a year after the murder when Barry George was first asked to give a statement. A search of his home disclosed an interest in the military. He was obsessed with celebrities and newscasters.

He was evasive in police interviews and lied that he had never heard of Jill Dando. It was Barry George and no other that murdered Jill Dando, he said. When you put all the evidence together when you look collectively at the component parts of it, each arising independently, then all this cannot be explained merely by unhappy coincidence. The investigation into the disappearance of Madeline

McCann was possibly the only case to receive more attention than Dando's murder.

Defence.

The defence closing address was surprisingly short. Clegg claimed that due to his low IQ of 75 Barry was incapable of the perfect crime which required meticulous planning. The only reason the prosecution said that Barry did it was that he was the person they arrested. He claimed that the only remaining forensic evidence, the polyester fibre, could just as easily have come from Alan Farthing, or Jill's wardrobe, or from somebody at the crime scene as the coat was left lying there on the ground for some hours after the murder.

I could not believe it was so short. I had expected a long powerful address. An awful sense of gloom descended on me and many supporters, which was reflected in e-mails and the websites guest book. We felt that the defence just did not measure up to our expectations. On Monday July 28 I asked the Met Police to reopen the Dando murder investigation if Barry was cleared, or to hold an inquiry if he was reconvicted.

I returned to London on Tuesday for the end of the trial. The judge gave his summing up on Wednesday. The following description is from my own notes.

Judges summing up

The jury would first have to decide if Susan Mayes saw Barry, and then if Richard Hughes and Mr Upfill-Brown saw the same man, who was dressed differently to the man seen by Mayes. If not they should acquit, there were obvious discrepancies. Exercise real caution, take special care, he said. He referred to the e-fit, the media, subconscious memory, passage of time etc.

Barry's beard. Only Hughes saw him at the live ID parade. A partial identification might be acceptable. Susan Mayes saw the man for ten seconds.

Terry Griffin the postman did not identify Barry as the man he saw on the day of the crime, but he did pick him as the man who approached him six weeks later. Has the incident any relevance?

The Bob Mills similarity in Hughes evidence. He and Upfill-Brown did not describe a Mediterranean appearance, as others had.

The six crimp marks on the bullet were hand punched, not of Eastern Bloc origin. It was unlikely that Barry could have converted the gun, he had a low I.Q. There was nothing in his flat to suggest that he had any converting skills, no tools etc.

The replica Bruni gun Barry owned could be converted.

Paramedics had cut Jill's raincoat off and left it lying on the ground, so the fibre was weak evidence. Her clothes had been disposed of so they could not be used to compare fibres in a TLC test. (Thin Layer Chromatology). Julia Moorhouse didn't see Barry with a bag though HAFAD staff had. Julia phoned the police at about 13.00 on the day of the crime. On the 26-2-2001 the police spoke to her after Barry had filed an alibi.

Barry's phone call at 12.32 to his service provider, the blurred yellow image on CCTV outside Fulham Football Ground.

HAFAD visit times. Rosario Torres first recalled a stressed out man with yellow clothes at about lunchtime. She heard Susan Bicknell saying 'I am having my lunch' at about 12.00. Barry had papers in a carrier bag. Leslie Symes also gave the time of his first visit at about 12.00.

His calling to Traffic Cars in an agitated state, and being driven to the Colon Cancer Centre.

His return two days later to HAFAD.

His conversation with Amanda Stocks about Jill Dando, Crimewatch, etc.

Regarding witnesses statements the judge asked were there two coats? Is DC John Gallagher's memory accurate? (Gallagher thought there might have been another coat similar to the Cecil Gee)

Barry was under police surveillance for twenty two days by seventy police officers. Two copies of the BBC's Ariel of April 27 1999 were found in his hallway. A third copy was found elsewhere.

His interest in guns, gun advertisements, military, the SAS, and military clothing.

Regarding lies told to the police about Jill Dando and guns, the judge pointed out that lies and false alibis are not indicative of guilt, and he explained how in the courts experience innocent people lie, maybe due to panic, or to improve a genuine innocence defence.

Are the prosecution correct in saying that he lied? Is his alibi a lie and if so does it matter?

There would be no pressure on time he told the jury before they retired to consider their verdict. Deliberations were to stop when they went on breaks. They should now elect a foreperson and try to reach a unanimous verdict.

The jury went out on Wednesday at 15.10. They came back at 15.50 asking for transcripts of Susan Mayes evidence at both trials. The judge ruled that the transcript of the first trial was not relevant. They were then sent home for the night unlike in 2001 when the jury was confined to a hotel.

I had a drink with Margaret that night. She said that she would only believe that Barry was free if she saw it herself. I told her to continue thinking like that, not to get her hopes up, be prepared for the worst and anything else would be a bonus.

On Thursday the judge read out Susan Mayes evidence and the video footage of her identifying Barry in 2000. I watched it with great interest and felt that she gave great consideration before picking him out. But I thought her quiet careful considerate manner was in marked contrast to her strident confidence when she gave her evidence in 2001.

When the jury were again sent home for the night I thought how like 2001 it all was, like it was all happening again. My optimism was slipping but Jeremy Moore said that I should have more faith in the defence. He seemed very confident.

Scott Lomax sent me a few text messages saying that Channel 4 would like to interview me after the verdict. I recalled Shulie Ghosh saying back in 2002 that she wanted to interview me when Barry was freed. I was interested but would not commit myself.

One day a reporter told me that there was something about Serj Sinclair's past. I mentioned that to Jeremy Moore who indicated that he was aware of it. In 2001 the then boyfriend of the black athlete Ashia Hansen was stabbed and it was claimed that it was a racist attack. Subsequently it was claimed that the incident was a set up to make money. The boyfriend was found guilty of staging the attack. He, Serj and another man were convicted of conspiracy to pervert the course of justice and were sentenced to two years imprisonment. The three appealed but were unsuccessful. My understanding is that Serj believes that they were miscarriage of justice victims.

On Friday morning I was met by Michelle and some of the MOJO people as I walked from Saint Paul's Underground Station to the court. I told them that I was meeting Scott in Nero's coffee shop but Tanya said that he was outside the Old Bailey. I wondered if she had already been to the court entrance why she was now with us in Newgate Street. Smelling a rat I separated from them, crossed the road and circled around behind the line of photographers who were massed outside the court. Only the Sun got a shot of me, an unflattering one of me standing chatting with Scott.

In the evening TV footage showed Michelle and the MOJO people as they approached in line. It was obviously well staged and I was glad that I avoided the trap.

We spent most of the morning sitting around in the cafeteria. The court was expected to finish early for the weekend. There would be no Saturday sitting this time. We were now seriously thinking that there could be a hung jury with the prospect of another retrial. It was a gloomy prospect as the prosecution usually come back stronger second time around.

During the lunch break Tanya Michelle and I discussed Susan Mayes evidence which still seemed the most damaging. I had been impressed by her slow and careful study of the video line-up and how she identified Barry. I thought that she was an honest witness, but that she was probably mistaken. Then to our surprise we were called down to Court Number One.

Aftermath

2008

When we left the Old Bailey's Court Number One I spoke briefly with John McVicar who seemed as surprised as I was. I guessed he would have needed to revise his next blockbuster, but in fact he wrote quite an accurate article for The Telegraph, though apparently not totally agreeing with the verdict.

I then phoned Margaret and asked her if she had heard any news, she hadn't. I told her it was over, that he was free. She asked me quietly if I should be saying that from the court and I realised that she couldn't take the news in. I called Michelle over and giving her my phone asked her to explain to Margaret. I then received a lot of congratulatory text messages from well wishers and supporters in the UK and Ireland. I tried to phone Tom but he was not at home. Another relative then told me that HMP Belmarsh had refused permission for me to visit Barry on Saturday as they had not been informed in time that I intended to visit. I was quite happy not to have to visit there again and I would not need their permission to see or speak to Barry in future.

I walked up to the cafeteria and got a cup of tea from the vending machine. Hamish Campbell was sat at a table working on his computer. I did not feel any sense of triumph, just relief that it was all over. Later as I sat alone outside the courtroom I was approached by reporter Amanda Perthen and we had a friendly chat.

After about an hour Michelle and I were led downstairs to where Barry and his legal team were waiting in a little room. Michelle hugged Barry and I shook hands with him, very formal like. He apologised to Michelle saying that he had his own media plans and so would not be going along with what she and MOJO had for him. Michelle said that was fine, whatever he wanted was ok. He then thanked me for all my support and apologised for sometimes having been angry with me.

There followed much confusion as to where Barry would go as none of us had been prepared for his release on that day. He couldn't go to East Acton I thought, that would be a disaster. Michelle and Mr Clegg seemed to think that the other had arranged something, and Mr Clegg said that he believed Michelle was looking after it. She then kindly offered to book him into a hotel if necessary. A taxi was coming for him but we didn't know where it was going. It was like something out of a Carry On film and I would have thought it funny if I were an outsider. Eight years trying to get him out and now we didn't know what to do with him.

Barry didn't seem to notice the apparent confusion such was his happiness and I suspect his disbelief that his ordeal was over. But his lawyers were anxious now for him to get away as quickly and quietly as possible. The taxi arrived.

'We need to move quickly' Clegg said. But now Michelle had a problem as she was expected to speak to the media out front.

'I will do that' Clegg said.

'I have been fighting this for the past 8 years, I *have* to speak', she replied.

Clegg looked dumbfounded and it appeared that Barry would be leaving without any family member with him. I had intended meeting Scott Lomax and perhaps speaking to Channel 4 but at the last minute Michelle asked me would I accompany Barry, so I did. But where were we going? Michelle phoned Serj and she then gave us the name of the Thistle City Hotel.

Barry and Doctor Susan Young were sat opposite me and a media solicitor Mr Wacks also shared the taxi. Mr Wacks explained his role to me, which was to represent Barry in relation to his media plans. I was facing the back window as the taxi sped towards the rear exit when I noticed Barry crouching down and putting his arms over his head. 'Stop that, no don't do that, you are not a criminal' Susan urged. I realised that photographers were closing in on us. As the taxi sped past one of them banged violently against the window next to Barry causing us all to jump. We raced up the street pursued by sprinting photographers but fortunately the traffic lights were in our favour and we sped away. I noticed a motorbike on our tail for a while but it was probably just a despatch rider. A photograph later published by the Daily Mail shows the tension etched on all our faces, we looked bloody awful. The unknown taxi driver did a brilliant job and asked no questions.

Many months later when I viewed Sky News footage I was amused that at the very moment when Michelle was expressing her heartfelt thanks to MOJO whose members were there with her on camera Susan Young, Mr Wacks and I were whisking Barry away in the dramatic dash to freedom, and no MOJO.

When our taxi arrived at the hotel Barry got out first and took a huge deep breath as if he was savouring his first taste of freedom. He apologised to the driver for any damage which might have been caused by the photographers and he picked up his transparent prison issue plastic bag which contained his belongings. I took the heavy bag from him and concealed it by draping my jacket over it as we made our way into the hotel lobby. We found a quiet spot and sat down apparently unnoticed. The atmosphere was electric; this was what we had fought for for over eight years. It was an amazing feeling. But it would not last for long.

I received a text from Susie Boniface asking me to tell Scott that the Sunday Mirror would like him to write an article for them. I forwarded the text to him and also told him that I would not now be doing the Channel 4 interview.

I asked Barry if he wanted a drink and he said that though not normally a drinker could he have a Pernod and Black on this occasion. I was a little taken aback thinking he would want a coke but Susan Young said one celebratory drink would be ok if sipped slowly. Then Michelle and some MOJO people including Serj arrived. Everybody seemed very happy at first and at about 16.30 I took a phone call from Scott. I asked him if he wanted to speak with Barry. Barry laughed when I said that somebody wanted to speak with him.

'Is it Scotland Yard' he asked?

'Half right Scot, Scot Lomax'.

Michelle and Tanya laughed and joked happily as Barry chatted with Scott.

The relaxed happy mood soon changed as Serj began engaging intensely with Mr Wacks. Mr Wacks had understood that he would be discussing media plans with Barry only in an unhurried relaxed manner over a few days but now Serj was saying that as it was Friday there was pressure to get something out for the Sunday papers. Mr Wacks was very annoyed at Serj's unexpected intrusion and expressed his unhappiness to me. Eventually a frustrated looking Serj said that all contracts were lost apart from one with the News of the World. That did not come as any surprise to me as I had been told by a contact some time earlier that just such a contract had been lined up and so I felt that these negotiations were just a smokescreen. The deal was done and it was just a matter of getting Barry to sign. I was dismayed to watch as his happy mood was replaced by a confused puzzled demeanour as he tried to make sense of the intense change which had come over all of us. I knew that things were now falling apart.

I found it hard to believe that they were again involving the News of the World after what had happened in 2001, like did they not learn anything from that?

I protested to Serj that we did not want that paper and told him about their 2001 headline 'The Imp Who Grew into a Devil', but he said that it was all that was left. I then took Barry to one side and said that I didn't mind what he did as long as it was his free choice. Susan Young then intervened and tried to reassure me that everything would be ok but I was not at all convinced, feeling that history was repeating itself. I was beat and could only hope that Mr Wacks would ensure that Barry's interests were looked after. Michelle, Serj and Mr Wacks then went to another part of the hotel where further negotiations took place; while I remained for a short time with Barry.

Meanwhile Margaret was at home alone and I thought somebody should go see her.

I managed to locate Michelle and told her I had to go to Margaret's. I said goodbye to Barry expecting that I would see him again soon, and I departed the hotel. I was in an unfamiliar part of London and had to walk around for a while before I located an Underground station.

On the train to East Acton I read on the Evening Standard that the guestbook on Michelle's website was inundated with congratulatory messages. I wondered if that referred to the JfB 'site, or was there another one which we were unaware of. Meanwhile I got more congratulatory texts from reporters in Ireland.

I phoned Margaret from the chip shop in East Acton saying that I would be around in a few minutes. 'Just yourself, are you alone' she asked? Was she expecting Barry to arrive with me I wondered? I got chicken and chips and went around. I noticed a packed overnight bag at the foot of the stairs.

'Cup of tea?'

'Ok, thanks'.

She said she could hardly believe the news. She told me that half a dozen reporters had been outside including Susie who had left a bottle of champagne. She quickly made the tea and then told me that Tanya was on the way in a car to take her to see Barry. Tanya soon arrived on foot with a list of clothes etc which Michelle had asked for. Shortly afterwards a large black limousine which had been hiding down the road while Tanya checked to see if the coast was clear arrived and they were gone.

Later after strolling aimlessly around East Acton for a while I celebrated our great *victory* alone with a pint in the Wishing Well. It was not the ending which I had dreamed of.

Team Barry

2008

Jill Dando was one of their own, and it would be naïve for anybody to think that the media would ever forgive Barry for the crime which he had been charged convicted and ultimately cleared of, unless perhaps the real killer was identified as in the Rachel Nickell case. If some of Barry's supporters expected a sympathetic reaction from them then they were sadly mistaken, and the immediate selling of his story to News International to the exclusion of others would not have helped matters.

On Saturday August 2 the Daily Mail reported that a 'police source' claimed that Alan Farthing and the Dando family wanted the murder case to remain closed. I thought that a little puzzling, if true.

Barry's 1982 victim's story was again published, 26 years after the event, for which Barry paid the price handed down by the courts.

The Telegraph claimed that a feud had erupted between Barry's supporters and Scotland Yard. William Clegg QC accused the police of 'closing their minds' to other suspects. He said the police and CPS needed to keep an open mind. 'I think they did close their minds after the arrest of Barry George, yes'.

Detectives were reported to be livid at the criticism. A Scotland Yard source said it was to be expected that people connected with George were now coming out to attack the police. Commander Simon Foy, head of the Met's Homicide Command said 'We are disappointed by today's verdict . . . however we respect the verdict of the court'.

I was quoted as saying that Barry would be like a fish out of water if he were to live in Ireland, and that he would not return to Fulham. Some East Acton neighbours said that they would be happy if he were to live with his mother there.

I do not agree that there is a feud with the police but I do believe that they missed something vital in the early days of the investigation. They may have placed too much reliance on the computer HOLMES rather then spending a little more time at the crime scene interviewing witnesses, preserving evidence, following up leads and kicking down doors without undue delay. I would call that constructive criticism.

It was pointed out by John McVicar that under Scottish law the jury would have had the option of a 'not proven' verdict. 'Not Proven' is basically an acquittal and was described in 1824 by novelist and Sheriff Sir Walter Scott as 'That bastard verdict, not proven'. I feel it was a little mean of McVicar to try and muddy the waters with such tripe, which has no relevance in English law. Barry was found Not Guilty. What could be clearer?

In the afternoon I met Scott for the last time in Victoria where we had an afternoon drink in the Shakespeare pub. At about 15.00 Michelle phoned me from the hotel saying that they had just finished the interviews and asked me what I was doing. I said I was with Scott but we could not talk further as the line went dead. At about 22.00 she again phoned me and asked if I knew that Scott had written an article for the Sunday Mirror. I explained that Scott was a writer and so it was to be expected that he might write something as he was also outside the Old Bailey when she and MOJO were speaking to the media. She said that Barry could lose money as a result and in the background I could hear him speaking quietly. But nobody had requested that I or Scott should remain silent. I later heard that there was consternation at the News of the World when it was realised that the Sunday Mirror was running a Barry George story ahead of their 'World Exclusive'. I had to laugh at that remembering the Clonakilty affair of July 2001. It wasn't revenge but it felt sweet nonetheless.

On Sunday morning I was listening to the radio and heard that just a few weeks prior to Jill Dando's death her agent Jon Roseman had finished writing a novel about a showbusiness agent whose male clients are murdered causing the agent to turn detective. The police interviewed Jon and the book titled GOOD MEN DIE LIKE DOGS was never published. I thought that was one weird story, stranger than fiction.

I went to a café with a couple of friends for breakfast, and bought a few newspapers.

The headlines hit me like a slap in the face. The News of the World article was prefaced with the warnings, OUR LAWYERS ARE WATCHING'. They described Barry as a 'BUG-EYED ODD-BALL.' They claimed he confessed: "I didn't kill Jill Dando-because I was stalking ANOTHER woman." He was shown posing with the horrible prison issue plastic bag which I had concealed when entering the hotel. In their 'World Exclusive' he was quoted as saying 'After leaving HAFAD I bumped into a woman who was later a prosecution witness and said I was stalking her . . . That was at 12.33pm . . .' That was obviously a reference to Julia Moorhouse who he had always denied meeting.

He denied being the man in the photo wearing a gas mask and brandishing a gun. At one time he had told me that it was him in the photo and at another he denied it. The police said that he had admitted to them during questioning that it was him and I accept that it was. He claimed to be a Leeds United fan since 1972 and I recall him saying to Eddie in the mid '70s that they were his favourite team. Eddie had laughed then thinking that he was a fan just because Leeds were then the league champions. Under the headline 'We didn't just nab the local nutter' retired detective inspector Ian Horrocks who was second in command of the murder investigation said he accepted the result of the retrial, but that he had agreed with the first jury's verdict. He claimed that they had carried out a thorough investigation and eliminated all suspects apart from one-Barry George.

The article then claimed that there was an uncomfortable incident at the hotel where Barry allegedly acted in a potentially indecent manner targeting Susan Young. (Dr Young would later confirm to me that she never once felt threatened or unsafe with Barry) In an article by Lucy Panton Susan was reported as being convinced that he was not capable of carrying out an execution killing.

As I looked over the papers I felt nauseous, broke out in a sweat and had to push my breakfast away, I felt quite ill and it was not Guinness related. Our great victory now seemed hollow and I later said to David James Smith that it seemed like we had won the battle but lost the war.

The Sunday Mirror 'Exclusive' had the independent article by Scott Lomax which was much more sympathetic towards Barry, though perhaps not entirely accurate. I was later told that there were threats of legal action over the article and I let it be known that if so I would be a witness for the defendants. Fortunately that Pandora's Box was never opened.

In the Mail on Sunday Jon Roseman revealed that he had never believed that Barry was the killer, instead thinking that Jill was shot by the Serbs.

Overall much of the press coverage seemed to insinuate that Barry got away with it, but that he was really guilty. That would seem to reflect the police response.

I saw just a little of the SKY News interview but I was not impressed by what I saw and heard. It seemed to me as if Barry was reciting from a script. I almost laughed as he earnestly said that he couldn't *begin* to understand what the Dando family was going through. It just didn't sound like something which he would say without being prompted, I felt they were not his words. I thought of the 'idiot cards' used by the BBC to prompt their interviewers on live shows such as 'Wogan' back in the mid '80s. David James Smith later described the interview as cringe making and I have to agree. Kay Burley appeared kind and sympathetic while Michelle smiled sweetly as Barry struggled to find the word 'foreman', prompted gently by Kay.

I felt that those media interviews were a mistake and damaged his chances of attaining public acceptance. Within two days he had been transformed from tragic miscarriage of justice victim deserving of some sympathy into something much less savoury. When I opened the JfB e-mails I saw nasty derogatory messages which were intended for Michelle, something which had rarely ever happened up to this. One told her to take her lovely brother to Ireland and to keep him there. That is the sanitised version. It was quite a contrast from the reaction which followed his 2007 victory in the appeal court.

I felt quite down in the dumps at the way things had suddenly turned around, and what should have been a joyful period at the successful end of the struggle instead seemed to have become sordid, unpleasant.

Later on that dreary Sunday I called around to Margaret's but she hadn't returned home. I dropped in a letter for Barry with some advice and offering him the opportunity of cooperating with this book but he never responded, I do not know if he even got to see it. Later another relative told me that Michelle Margaret and Barry were going away for a while to an undisclosed location. That night I endured a horrible ear bashing from a person on the outer fringes of the family who said that the latest jury's verdict did not convince him.

It was with a sense of relief that I left London to go home on Monday, with 48 trips to the UK including 36 prison visits behind me.

I was pleased to read along the way that there would be a police review of the case by the Met but I would have preferred if an outside force were to conduct it.

After I got home I read in some paper that Barry and family were on the Isle of Wight where Michelle introduced him to Sion Jenkins. The IPCC needed to know if I wanted to pursue my complaint but I did not now wish to have any further involvement and so I dropped it.

Eaten bread is quickly forgotten and I and my fellow supporters were discarded. I felt quite bitter about it for a long while, and I was not alone in feeling like that. Some people put their professional reputations on the line and got no thanks.

Scott later told me that JfB's website had received 978 hits on Friday August 1, 533 on Saturday, and 369 on Sunday. On October 11 I shut it down.

It was now open season on Barry and the press set about destroying any hope of him settling into any kind of normal life in his home city of London.

I watched dispassionately as his reputation, such as it was, nosedived over the last days of 2008 under a welter of tabloid fantasy. They ran stories on what he ate, what bookshops he visited, his temporary accommodation. They claimed incorrectly that he was stalking a nurse, that Sky's Kay Burley was frightened sick by him, that he was interested in Cheryl Cole of X Factor, that he was involved with the partner of a convicted killer etc. To make things even better a 'spokesman' for him allegedly confirmed some of those manufactured stories. Pat Reynolds said to me one day: 'with friends like those who needs enemies?' It was a little sad to see the end results of the long hard battle and one day a despairing Margaret said to me that it was now worse than when he was in prison.

In an October 10 feature in the Daily Mail David Jones summed up the whole sorry state of affairs. He described how Jill's grave had been a haven of peace for Jack Dando, aged 90, and her brother Nigel, but that now Barry was planning to visit it.

Singh Clair, described as Barry's spokesman confirmed that. Nigel Dando said that he would not object to the visit: 'It might give Mr George cause to ponder and reflect', he said. The article described how others in 'Team Barry' included his sister, his mother, friend Robert Charig, and Sion Jenkins was described as a fringe member. Then there was the body charged with monitoring Barry and smoothing his path back into society under a Multi Agency Public Protection Agreement. (MAPPA)

In an e-mail to David Michelle had claimed that Barry was the victim of a media-driven plot designed to smear and intimidate him. I was quoted as saying that I feared that the police, having ultimately failed to nail him for the murder might try to frame him. 'It could be like OJ Simpson, you get him second time around.' Margaret was quoted as saying 'how can he be happy when their all out to get him.' I was quite correctly described as being estranged from the main George camp for suggesting that the MOJO outfit might be self-serving.

Mr Singh Clair was described as a Midlands-based freelance journalist who was enlisted by MOJO to promote George's cause four years earlier. That bit of news explained a lot to me, Serj would seem to have been merely doing what he had been hired for.

Robert Charig told David that Barry had said that his ex wife Itsuko Toide had sent him tender messages. Serj denied the claim but said that there was somebody new, that they had met a few times. 'She's about the same age as Barry—and he's very excited about it. But I'm always cautious of these people because she obviously knows who Barry is and that he's going to get a lot of money. He's been advised to be careful and keep himself in check. We don't want him in some kind of trap.'

David concluded his article: 'Perish the thought. For the Dando's family sake, we must hope that Barry Michael George receives similarly sound advice before he boards the train to Weston-Super-Mare, armed with a big bouquet.'

I and some of Barry's former supporters began to fear that the press attention would one day result in him reacting in some way to the harassment which would give the police a reason to lock him up again and so on October 13 2008 I reluctantly contacted MOJO to suggest that he get help or counselling or I would again become his regular visitor, 'inside' again.

Observation and Analysis

Do the powers that be really want to solve the Jill Dando case? Barry George is quite rightly seeking compensation for his eight years in prison. If the case was finally solved it might bolster his case. For that reason only I would like to see the compensation issue conclusively resolved, lest it be an impediment to progress.

I do continue to have an interest in the unsolved murder; given the turmoil it caused me and my family. I have been in contact with the powers that be over the years and as recently as 2012 I have raised concerns at the highest level of the British Government in the hope of reinvigorating the investigation.

'If Barry did not kill Jill Dando then who did?' That question was first aired to me by Margaret Renn back in 2002 prior to the first appeal. I have seen it repeated oft times since. Of course we now know that Barry is innocent of that crime but let us look at the final part of the question: WHO DID?

On 19 March 2000 Hamish Campbell said in an Observer interview that the most likely options for the killer knowing that Jill Dando would be in Gowan Avenue were that Jill had told someone that she would be there, that they in turn had told somebody else, that the killer lived in the street, or that the killer decided after observation and analysis that by just waiting there he would eventually get her.

Mr Campbell may have been correct in that line of thinking.

Let's have a look at those Observer points in the light of what we now know.

In 2002, nearly a year after Barry George's conviction written evidence emerged which undermined the Crown's 2001 position that only Jill's fiancé and her agent were aware of her intention to visit Gowan Avenue on the day of her death. That position was revised in 2008 to *only those closest to her knew.* That is an important change and opens the possibilities quite a bit. So how might the killer have known she would be in Gowan Avenue that day?

Who can say that Jill or somebody close to her did not inadvertently perhaps reveal her plans for the day? In the early afternoon she was due to attend a fashion event in Hyde Park's Lanesborough Hotel, along with a friend. She had booked the tickets a few weeks earlier. Gowan Avenue is mid way between Chiswick and the Lanesborough and so was on her route. A conversation with her agent that morning about her faulty fax machine gave confirmation that she was on her way and a hacker or eavesdropper could have picked that up.

Jill would talk to people, she was newsworthy and information would leak to the media, or perhaps to others.

Could the killer have lived in the street? John McVicar speculated on that and anything is possible. We know that Jill's was a familiar face in the locality and neighbours would know if she was home by seeing her car or hearing the alarm zapper or encountering her in the shops or street. People knew where she lived; it was not a secret address. There were some in the locality who admitted to hating her, and it would seem that a certain type of person also hated her as was apparent by internet postings following her death.

There is at least one odd aspect to the murderer's departure. Why close the gate when leaving the crime scene? It has been suggested to me that it was a mistake done as a matter of routine by somebody who perhaps regularly visited the house, the unconscious habit of a neat and tidy person.

On observation and analysis, phone calls e-mails and text messages are not as secure as we would like, as many have found to their cost. On 25 July 1999 the UK Independent's Sophie Goodchild revealed an extraordinary security lapse where BT Cellnet allowed an investigative reporter to gain access to a number of peoples voice mail boxes. She simply claimed that she had lost her phone but was expecting an important message. She was supplied a pin code which allowed her access to her voice mail, and (with their permission) she accessed the messages of fifteen other people. She potentially had access to five million accounts; all she needed were their phone numbers and the confidential pin code which she was given.

We know that Jill was of interest to the so called 'Utility Stalker' who tried to access her phone gas and water accounts, and according to court evidence somebody was phoning around to J Dando numbers which were in the phone directory. So who was watching Jill?

Were there some who feared damage to reputations if Jill had actually written the book she spoke of, or if the Utility Stalker published a 'kiss and tell' story so beloved of the sleazier elements of the media? Had she lived then that was a real possibility, but in death she was elevated to a higher plane and such stories would have been untouchable.

Jill may have been the subject of observation and analysis in the run up to her death though that may have been carried out in a more sophisticated way than the Crown suggested, i.e. by hanging around in the street running the risk of attracting attention, or by lying in wait behind the small hedge in a cramped position. Jill discussed details of her plans for the fateful Monday a few days prior to her death while she was working in Dublin. It is quite possible that she discussed her plans with more than one person, and so her visit to Gowan Avenue could have become known to many more people than originally thought.

There are a number of theories as to who might have killed Jill. Perhaps a jealous former lover, somebody upset by BBC Crimewatch, Scottish crime gangs, the Serbs, someone from her past upset over some personal row, or a 'stranger murder', i.e. carried out at random by a stalker or opportunist for no apparent reason.

Towards the end of 1999 when the first Dando investigation appeared to be dead in the water the focus switched to the 'stranger murder' theory and Barry George was dragged into the frame. The rest is history and the police still appear to believe they were correct. Perhaps the lessons of the Rachel Nickell investigation should be heeded where killer Robert Napper was ruled out until advances in DNA evidence proved otherwise, leaving an innocent man branded as her killer for many years.

Regarding the much vaunted Serb theory there may be some merit in that due to the Kosovo war, Jill's TV appeal and the NATO bombing of Radio Television Serbia which killed 16 TV workers. Jill's TV appeal was widely seen as taking the Albanian side in the Kosovo conflict. Tony Blair justified the bombing of Radio Television Serbia saying it was a mouthpiece of Serbian propaganda. The UK International Development Secretary Clair Short declared that it was a 'legitimate target'. For every action there is a reaction. Jill met her death three days later. She was seen as the Face of BBC, which in turn was seen as the mouthpiece of Britain. So as a result she could have been seen as a 'legitimate target'.

On the other hand she could have been shot in an attempt to discredit the Serbs, a possibility which was referred to at Barry's 2001 trial. In times of war truth is the first casualty and anything is possible.

However, the method of execution seems to have been very personal, hands on using a makeshift gun. That is seen as unusual. The phone calls to the BBC following the murder may have been a smokescreen to divert the police from the real killer who had no connection to the former Yugoslavia. The caller may not have been the actual killer and hopefully the police will have explored anything that voice analysis might have thrown up.

Would somebody try and erect such a smokescreen? The answer is maybe, somebody could. It happened in Northern Ireland, 1991, when Greenfinch soldier Susan Christie killed army officer's wife Penny McAllister in a planned attack and then claimed that a wild bearded man had attacked them both. The RUC police quickly uncovered the truth.

It happened again in 2009 in Dublin when Eamon Lillis killed his 'Bond Girl' wife Celine Cawley with a blow of a brick during a personal row, and then claimed that they were attacked by a masked man. An innocent man was duly questioned but the Garda soon uncovered the truth.

Killers quite often try to frustrate the police investigation, by faking suicide or pretending that somebody else was responsible.

People interested in unsolved murder cases often have their own theories as to who the killer might be. A little knowledge is a dangerous thing and we shouldn't jump to conclusions but there is an angle which causes me to look in a certain direction though all I see is a high brick wall. Numerous questions have been asked by me to the Met Police under freedom of information questioning the thoroughness of some aspects of the investigation. The answers are always vague and one has to try and interpret them. If a defendant answered in a similar fashion they would be seen as evasive.

The answers seem to indicate that not everybody who should have been considered as suspect was, and that alibis were accepted without thorough checking.

Unfortunately it appears that having belatedly investigated Barry George and deciding that he was their man the police went down a cul-de-sac and as was apparent by their statements immediately following the acquittal in 2008 are now reluctant to admit they got it wrong.

It is quite possible that Jill knew her killer and did not see any immediate threat to her safety. Her scream was described by witness Richard Hughes as sounding like somebody surprising somebody, not significant. That 'somebody' took time to close the gate after shooting Jill. Forensic testing of the gate does not appear to have revealed anything significant even though the police believe the killer was not wearing gloves. Could the *absence* of a strangers DNA be in itself significant?

I have long believed that a fresh team with no axe to grind or reputation to defend should be asked to carry out a thorough review and investigation.

It is still possible for this case to be properly solved, if the will is there. The police and CPS should go back, re-evaluate the crime, the first twenty four hours, given what they now know. If it was a random murder carried out by an opportunist then it is unlikely that it will be solved. However, if it were a planned killing then it is still possible to solve it. Now that the way seems open for Serbia to join the EU maybe the British Government could do as they did in relation to Bulgaria and Georgi Markov and send detectives to Serbia to investigate. And perhaps the police should look again at all those who knew or could reasonably assume that Jill would be calling to her house on that day. As I said earlier, the closing of the gate suggests familiarity.

Finally I would say compare and contrast statements made in 1999/2000 with subsequent statements, interviews assertions or publications, and double check alibis.

God is in the detail if one digs deep enough.

Epilogue

I returned to London in December 2008 on a private visit. In an odd way I missed the old days, the sense of purpose. While I was there a jury returned an open verdict on the Jean Charles de Menzes case.

On the 18th the Rachel Nickell case finally ended with the conviction of Robert Napper.

A week later my brother who first informed me of Barry's involvement died. That was a sad event but it was good that he saw the shame of the murder conviction lifted from our family.

Jack Dando died on his birthday aged 91 on February 15 2009 without seeing justice for his daughter.

Shannon went to sleep for the last time on 23 June 2009 aged 15. I found that quite difficult to deal with.

Mike Burke

Barry sued the papers for their untrue allegations about him and won substantial compensation from a number of them including the News of the World. I must confess to a feeling of Schadenfreude following the demise of that publication in 2011.

I met Barry again in September 2011 following the death of his mother while she was on holiday in Limerick. Barry was still the same Barry I have always known; he hadn't grown horns or become a monster as some of the Free Press would have us believe. He asked me then if I could clarify that he did not deliberately break off contact with me in 2008 which I am happy to do.

Bibliography

Appeal Court Approved Judgement 2008.

All About Jill. David James Smith.

Dead on Time. How and Why Barry George murdered Jill Dando.

John McVicar

Forensics. Dr Zakaria Erzinclioglu

GCHQ.

Google Internet Search

Kosovo Jim Judah

Thirty six murders and two immoral earnings. Ludovic Kennedy.

Justice for Jill. Scott Lomax.

Memoirs of a Radical Lawyer. Michael Mansfield QC

Teenage Barry with dog Scamp and Michelle and Mother

Barry, Michelle with baby and Mother.

Me, Margaret and Barry in HMP Whitemoor, a famous photo,
which caused the row.

Monument in Wormwood Scrubbs to the three murdered policemen.

Paddy Joe Hill, founder of
MOJO.

Newspaper cutting of leaving the Old Bailey in a taxi with Dr Susan
Young, Barry and me . . . escaping the press.

Printed in Great Britain
by Amazon